The End of Freud?

The End of Freud?

by Edward Nersessian

International Psychoanalytic Books (IPBooks)
New York • http://www.IPBooks.net

Published by IPBooks, Queens, NY
Online at: www.IPBooks.net

Cover art by Kathy Kovacic, Blackthorn Studio

Interior Design & Layout by Noel S. Morado

ISBN: 978-1-969031-13-7

To Mary,
Without whose support and
encouragement I could have
never been able to complete
this 10 year voyage.

Contents

Prologue

247 East 82nd Street in Manhattan, New York is the home of one of the oldest and most renowned psychoanalytic institutes in the United States, older even than the national American Psychoanalytic Association (APsA). The building was purchased in 1946, a number of years after the institute had been in existence. It was considered the mecca of psychoanalysis and had some of the best internationally known names in its roster of psychoanalysts, a number of them refugees from Europe during the second world war. A few of its members became president of APsA over the years, and helped establish the standards of education both internationally and locally. I will detail later the rigorous nature of the training at NYPSI.

In the fifties, sixties, seventies and to some degree eighties and nineties, when psychoanalysis and Freud's "discoveries" occupied an important role in psychiatry, in literature, in philosophy and in the treatment of psychological conditions, the institute was a place for rigorous education and vigorous debate and it had a certain aura of exclusivity and specialness around it. There was no dearth of qualified applicants, until the eighties mostly physicians, and saw itself as educating students in understanding the mysteries of being human, or more accurately the psychology of humans.

It was the most classical Freudian institute in the U.S., and from what I observed during my years being active in the International Psychoanalytic Association, also in the world, or at least the part of the world where psychoanalytic training was present.

It was and is my institute and it has changed. I will describe the changes later in this book, but importantly the changes have very much to do with where Freud's ideas and theories are today. Using a mix of autobiography and theory, I plan to assert that the end of Freud has come. Perhaps this is not new, but I try to show the problem with his theories from the perspective of someone who was a classical psychoanalyst. The parts of the book that deal with theory are inevitably somewhat dry as they resemble talks given to psychoanalysts or papers written for that audience. For that I apologize.

Finally, I should say when I talk or write about the end of Freud, I mean it in a very specific way, that is to say, his theories about mental functioning are mostly wrong. However, Freud wrote a great deal and his ideas are interesting and even at times quite illuminating. They go beyond the narrow field of psychoanalytic treatment and therefore they deserve to be read and discussed and debated. Like works of philosophy, poetry, literature and music, they have a forever quality. My critique only applies to the use of his theories to treat psychological ailments.

CHAPTER 1

Childhood Years

The two pictures hung on the western wall, near the window facing the garden.

They were there all through my life in Tehran. I left in 1960, age 15.

Fifty-five years later, I read the story my mother wrote about her life. I had it in my possession for 10 years. She writes about her little son asking her about the boys in the pictures. They are your brothers she responds. The little boy asks if they are my brothers, where are they? At school she responds.

When you go away to school you don't come back. Except for three brief visits, I never went back to Tehran.

The same week I found my mother's notes while reorganizing my office files, I also found my father's papers. In the early 1920's, my father who came from a titled and land owning family, was declared "voiceless" in Armenia, a term that was used to describe his having lost all his civil rights. As the years passed, he witnessed more and more of his properties seized by the communist government. An Armenian historian Bagrat Borian (Wikipedia) described it this way:

"The Revolutionary Committee started a series of indiscriminate seizures and confiscations, without regard to class, and without taking into account the general economic and psychological state of the peasantry. Devoid of revolutionary planning, and executed with needless brutality, these confiscations were unorganized and promiscuous. Unattended by disciplinary machinery, without preliminary propaganda or enlightenment, and with utter disregard of the country's unusually distressing condition, the Revolutionary Committee issued its orders nationalizing food supply of the cities and peasantry. With amazing recklessness and unconcern, they seized and nationalized everything – military uniforms, artisan tools, rice mills, water mills, barbers' implements, beehives, linen, household furniture, and livestock."

As my father watched the seizure of his properties, he also began to witness the arrest and deportation of certain Armenians. On one of his lands there was a chapel which had been built by an errant monk, and which had become a place of worship for villagers in the larger surrounding area. The existence of this chapel increased the threats on my father and in 1929 He finally decided to escape to Iran. He hoped to return a few months later when he believed all the instability and danger would subside and a more logical order would take hold. With the help of Kurdish mountaineers, he and a few others attempted the escape. A couple turned back after a few days of extremely harsh travel which took place at night, and the remaining despite some air assault, severe thirst, hunger and cold managed to reach the Iranian border in or near Maku.

By that point the Kurdish guides had taken from them all their money and most of their belongings including clothes and my father entered Iran only with a few gold coins he had well-hidden on himself.

After finding a place to live with some other refugees, he sold his gold coins and bought grape. He made wine and sold it and for some years he lived this way as he saw his chances of ever returning home fade away.

Years passed and on the recommendation of a person he had met in Maku he was introduced to the local construction manager of Skoda Company, to provide cement for a project. Over time this turned into work for Skoda as they did different projects in Northern Iran and led eventually to his moving to Tehran and striking on his own in the construction business.

When the war began, he was in Tehran and in the summer of 1941 some of his acquaintances found out about his oldest son's death at the Russian front, since Armenia was under Russian control and young Armenians were drafted into the Russian army. Melikset was only 16. When my father left his native village of *Rehanloo,* he had left behind three sons, the youngest a toddler. His friends withheld the news from him though in his autobiography he writes about a dream that Fall in which his son is killed by the Russians as he tries to escape. He finds out in January that his son was killed in the war and his wife had died within a short few months from a "weak heart" aggravated by grief.

In 1943 there is a line in his notes which reads as follows: "I had been alone too long and decided to marry a girl, Violette, and soon I had a son Edik (short for Edvart)". A little over two years later he had another son, Vahe.

I was delivered by a midwife who believed strongly in increasing the defense system of the body by exposing the infant to fresh air. At three o'clock in the morning of December 1, 1944 she delivered me and immediately held me outside the window to boost my defenses. Winter's in Teheran can be very cold and this particular night it had been snowing. My father and my middle maternal uncle had been driving around the clinic in a carriage waiting for the news of my birth and they talked about how cold that winter was. The midwife unfortunately did not succeed in boosting my defenses but instead I developed pneumonia. The theory which seemed to be accepted by many, since she was much sought after and had her own clinic, did not work for me. By the end of fifth grade I had measles, chicken pox, whooping cough, scarlet fever, diphtheria, mumps and typhoid fever, the last one almost killed me, a fact that probably left its marks on my psyche. My brother on the other hand, despite the fact that we were very close and playmates, did not seem as vulnerable to infections and only contracted diphtheria.

I grew up happy, thanks to a very caring, loving, involved, ambitious and occasionally moody mother. The one source of unhappiness and occasional anxiety was my father's absences, while extremely loving, indulgent and proud of us, he was frequently away on work, sometimes for long periods of time. By long I mean up to six months. By the time I knew about what he did for work, he had his own company that build roads in Iran. I am proud of the fact that he was the first person to introduce Caterpillar to the construction industry in Iran by purchasing his first Caterpillar Graders. Bulldozers, Loaders etc. were to follow. There was always, however, an air of mystery in my younger years about my father's past and the family in Armenia. While he spoke about them to my mother, he rarely spoke about them or his past with us. I don't even know if my mother knew everything; he was very intent on protecting us. His autobiography remains the main source of information about him along with the odds and ends we learnt when in Armenia. For instance one of my half brother's, Grigor, when we visited them told me about how my father's family had been mistreated after his escape and how the local government did everything to prevent Grigor from going to engineering school and how they even made it harder afterwards regarding his work. Then there was the episode of this man named Hamo, who suddenly appeared in our lives in Tehran when I was 9 or 10 and became very friendly with my father's two best friends and then with my father. He came to dinner to our home at least two to three times a month and somehow I heard he was a friend of a general in Iran. Yet, he had just come to Iran, which must have been in a clandestine manner. Then one day he disappeared and some years later, again from hearing bits and pieces of conversation I realized he had been a spy, sent to Tehran to spy on people like my father. When I met my half brother's, they told me he had done them harm upon his return to Armenia but did not offer details.

Back to my upbringing, since I am a psychoanalyst I went through my own analysis in the seventies and spoke about the fact that my mother sent me to nursery school with French nuns who had Italian names (*soeur Gestina* and *soeur Gina Rosa*) when I was two and a half years old, few months after my brother's birth. When in 1976 I asked my mother, she said no I was in fact three and a half. I was at the time trying to understand why I had cried so much on the first day when they took me to the nursery and why the only threat that made me agree to enter the building was that if I did not go in, they would give my uniform to another child. My uniform was a white overall with a red bow tie. My explanation based on my original assumption was that I was reacting to being sent away so soon after the birth of my brother specially because I had been told that I was not weaned from the breast until close to his birth. The correction by my mother weakened that explanation without fully eliminating it. Then, when almost at seventy I discovered my mother's notes and read about her answer to me that my brothers, in the pictures, were away at school, I thought maybe my anxiety was connected to a childish interpretation that you don't come back home when you go to school, no wonder, I did not want to enter the school building on that first day only.

The nursery school was followed by one year at "College Saint-Louis" established by French priests in Tehran in 1862, then three years at Mademoiselle Marika school and then back to College Saint-Louis until the end of ninth grade.

I was, I must admit, somewhat spoilt. Unlike some of the other children, my mother insisted in taking me to school herself, and as I complained about the food for lunch that she was sending me to school with, she offered, or I insisted, I don't recall, to come and get me at school, go back home, make me a fresh lunch and then take me back to school. She made the journey to my school and back, about a 2 miles distance, 6 times a day.

My mother was born in Sari in the province of Mazandaran. Her father, Hayrabet, was a caretaker for the properties and lands of Reza Shah in the area. His parents had emigrated to Iran from Azerbaijan. My mother's mother Nvart, was very young around 18 when she got married and had my mother shortly afterwards. Within two years she had my aunt Nina followed by two boys. When the youngest child was about a year old, she became pregnant again and they decided she should abort which they mistakenly called a curettage which essentially meant using a needle to burst the amniotic sac and cause a miscarriage. As was often the case with this procedure, an infection ensued and death followed. I think she was at most 27 when she died. My mother was 8 and she was pulled out of school to watch over the other children. A few years later my grandfather remarried. His new wife was not very much loved by my mother and her siblings though when I was growing up my parents supported my step grandmother and her two grown up children for some years and she was often in our house and very caring towards me. My mother as a result of her early loss developed a very independent and resilient character. She was known to ride on horse back from their town to the various villages where Reza Shah had his properties. Nevertheless it must have been difficult for her given my father was so frequently away. I remember, one time when he was stuck in northern Iran where he had a project and could not even send us money as those days the notion of a woman having a bank account was non existent, my having a temper tantrum complaining that I could not it pickled pork for another day. But always the difficult times would end, my father would arrive with all sorts of goodies and life would go back to normal. Despite an absence of formal education, my mother had a love for reading and taught herself to read Armenian and later Farsi. When she ended up after 1978 in New York where she spent the last years of her life, she learnt to speak English well enough to manage all her daily activities. She would come to my home from her apartment 3 blocks away and spend a couple of ours there every day. Sundays we would go to her for dinner until she was too old to cook for all of us and she began to come to us Sunday nights. One Sunday night in 2005 she did not show up at the usual time which she kept like a clockwork. After her phone did not answer, we went to her apartment and found her lying on the floor next to her bed unresponsive. She had not been ill but I guess she either had a massive stroke or more likely a heart attack. She was 82.

I was a good student and first in my class. Mlle. Marika was very demanding and eager to maintain a high standard in her school. She was quadriplegic, having been shot in her spine by a boyfriend she did not want any more. She was wheelchair bound with her head leaning all the way right resting on her shoulder. She rarely if ever praised and always found a shortcoming no matter how well you did your homework. The other teachers were strict but soft compared to her. She was also demanding about cleanliness, neatness and order. Your work had to be always well presented. Because she could not hold a book, she would ask one of the students to hold the book while she read the lessons for the class. More than once she told me off in class for my nails that were too long and dirty. She would say tell your mother to cut your nails in front of all the students and the school was co-ed. In many ways she was quite tough. At the end of the second grade when I scored 10 out of ten on all my subjects both in French and in Farsi, at the parent teacher meeting with my parents she told them "don't get too excited, in a country when everyone is blind, the one with one eye is king". This has stayed with me all my life. My good grades and being first in the class, did not however, continue. After I had typhoid fever in the fifth grade, the year I won many prizes, my grades began to fall in the sixth to the ninth grade. I did ok but not well, to what degree the trauma of the illness with the threat of death had affected me, or was it the effect of puberty, I would never know.

Life as a boy in Tehran was quite enjoyable. I had two sets of friends those from school and those from the neighborhood I lived in. From about the 4th grade, most of my weekends, holidays and most afternoons were spent with my brother and the boys in the neighborhood playing soccer and riding our bikes. We played soccer in the street where we lived. Not too many cars passed through our street those days and so the street was our soccer field.

At home most weekends relatives came over for long lunches, my aunts, uncles, friends. My parents were always the hosts. In the summer, sometimes the get together would take place out of the city. We would go to a stream near the mountains and have a picnic. As kids we would play in the water or try to climb the lower reaches of the mountains. The women would set up the food, the men do the kebabs. There was always plenty of vodka to drink and most of the men would fall asleep after lunch. The women would lie down, not sleep and chat. Kids would play.

It is only with puberty my interests changed and the soccer playing in the street was replaced by listening to Elvis Presley, Bill Haley, Everly Brothers and others. Along with this, came the interest in girls and dance parties. I had had a crush in second grade for a girl but now it was more about which girls' parents would allow their daughter to come to one of the guys homes for dancing parties. Getting dressed up in what we then considered fashionable, tight tapered pants with a slit near the ankle, so called pegged legs, and shirts with a band that you wore over the trousers and copying Elvis' style when he danced became the pre-occupation and the activity that drew the most interest and therefore less was devoted to studying.

In sum, I had a happy childhood and early adolescence despite my many illnesses. My father's periodic long absences were the only dark clouds except one other sad event from when I was around ten years old. It is about this young cousin of my aunt, Armen, who appeared in our life at that point. He had been living in Sari in Northern Iran, and then he moved to the city for work. He was an engineer. Handsome, young, very friendly, he started hanging out with my youngest aunt who was still single. He would come to our house where my aunt lived most of the time and have dinner with us, go to the movies with her, occasionally taking me also, and everyone liked his presence. He even taught me how to do crossword puzzles. About a year after moving to Tehran he met a girl and soon they were engaged. At this point his company began sending him to construction sites in other provinces. I remember quite vividly coming home from school one day, eager to read the latest Tintin comic book I had borrowed from a classmate, and my grandmother opening the door with tears in her eyes. She told me Armen had died. For the next days our house was a very sad place, the air became heavy and it seemed like all the lights had dimmed. Armen had been on an assignment and on the worksite he had suddenly lost consciousness and died before they could get him to the nearby hospital. The cause, I was told, was bleeding in his brain. Years later as a doctor I realized he had had a cerebral aneurysm. To this day I remember a beautiful Tehran night with the moon and the stars shining and on the terrace in our home, Armen and my youngest aunt Bibik dancing the swing to Tennessee Ernie Ford's *Sixteen Tons*. I had never seen this kind of dancing or heard this type of music before, and I was enthralled. Perhaps it was the precursor to my becoming so taken by Elvis and Rock and Roll, though preceding the Elvis period I had seen "Seven Brides for Seven Brothers" five times.

Mlle. Marika's school only went to the end of the 4th grade. So, after finishing there I went back to College Saint–Louis where I had been for first grade, and my parents had felt it was not rigorous enough. College Saint-Louis was located in an old building in a small street in Tehran, it had a large courtyard surrounded by four buildings. Every morning we gathered in the courtyard and the French national anthem was played, and the flag was raised. I no longer remember if both the Iranian anthem and the Marseillaise were played or just one.

School began at 8 and ended at 5. Unlike Iranian schools however, we did not have class on Sundays, so we had Fridays and Sundays off as opposed to Wednesday afternoon and Friday.

Persian history, geography of Iran, and Persian literature and poetry were taught in Farsi; everything else was in French. We had the main Persian holidays off, plus Christmas and Easter Monday, and July and August. A few times in the summer we went to the coast or, one time, to a spa town, but most of the time we were in Tehran. I would hang out with my brother and friends in the morning, most of the time stay in—due to the heat from lunch until about five pm—and then again hangout until about eight. Most people, including those in my family, had a siesta after lunch but I was not able to, so I read. I read Persian books—novels but also translations such as Sherlock Holmes, French books, and, when I started taking after-school English classes in 6th or 7th grade, English books. I read the *Count of Monte Christo* in French, for a very long time a favorite of mine. I also discovered Mickey Spillane and when I was able, I started reading his works in English. I enjoyed mysteries enormously, but the occasional naughty scenes were also an attraction. My love of mysteries was such that the summer before starting medical school I read all the Agatha Christies I could get my hands on.

Saint-Louis only went to the end of the 9th grade when you took the French *Brevet d'Etudes* Primaries and then, one either went to a French high school or a Persian high school. My parents—primarily my father—decided to send my two-and-a-half-year-younger brother and me to boarding school in England.

Before closing this chapter, a word about my choice of becoming a doctor. Aa I began to recover from Typhoid fever, I began to collect all the empty bottles of the various medications I was taking, and some I had taken and, in the afternoons when everybody would be having a siesta, I would organize the bottles and play at being a doctor dispensing various medicines for various illnesses. This lasted only a few months but looking back, it may have been an early determinant of my decision to go to medical school.

CHAPTER 2

Moving Into Adulthood

My mother, my brother, and I left Tehran on a beautiful summer day. Most of my aunts, uncles, and cousins came to the airport to say goodbye. I felt excitement and anticipation mixed with a touch of sadness. Seeing my father cry for the first time in my life made me recognize that we were embarking on a journey that would change our life.

After a stop in Beirut and one in Geneva, the plane landed at Heathrow which, due to construction work, looked like barracks—a huge contrast compared to the recently built, beautiful Mehrabad airport. I comforted myself by thinking that once we left this dingy, depressing area we will encounter beautiful London. It was a foggy, cloudy, rainy day and the sight of all black soot-covered buildings soon dissuaded me of that illusion. It was dreary, gloomy and cold. The guardian my parents had hired was apparently on vacation, and a young aide met us and took us not to a nice hotel but to a bed and breakfast on Cromwell road. They put the three of us in one cold room with no bathroom and, not being accustomed to putting money to have the gas fire work, we sat there shivering and wondering if we should take the next flight back to Tehran. This was 1960 and it soon became evident to me that the damage done by the Second World War had not been repaired, and England was a poor, somewhat devastated place.

It is fortunate that a family that we only barely knew in Tehran, was staying at the same place with two sons, one my age and one my brother's age, and so we were able to gradually, over the next few days, make peace with what seemed like our misfortune. However, things began to change as the other boy and myself found out that another friend of mine who had already spent a year in London was in town and before long the three of us were hanging out in Piccadilly Circus, Leicester Square with its many movie houses and specially Soho and its strip clubs.

When the guardian returned from his vacation, we met with him. He was an Armenian and a totally unimpressive man who did not give the impression that you could trust him. He informed us that we will be meeting the headmaster of the school in a restaurant for afternoon tea, two days before we were scheduled to leave for school. The meeting at the restaurant near Kings Cross station, from where we travelled two days later, was uneventful and awkward. We knew nothing about afternoon tea rituals and of course did not speak much English. I was the only one who spoke some and I struggled through with some help from the guardian. The main take away from the meeting was to arrange to meet for the train trip to Harrogate and an offer from the headmaster that my mother could rent a room in the apartment of the school secretary across the street from the school, with the proviso that she could not see us except for a relatively short visit on the weekend. By the time we left London, however, I had developed an affection for the city and was sorry to leave it.

The train ride from London to Harrogate impressed me. I had never been on what seemed to me like a super fancy train before, where they even served lunch. But that ride also delineated the fancy from the drab for when we arrived by taxi from the train station in Harrogate to Norwood college, fancy ended. Norwood college sat at the corner of Leeds road which connected Harrogate to Leeds and a secondary street. It was an L-shaped large building with two or three entrances. The entrance we took immediately brought us into a grey, shabby hallway with a stale odor leading to stairs which took us two floors up to our dorm rooms. My room was small with only a small window on the top of one of the walls. The feeling of walking up those stairs and then into this room was shock, surprise, dread, regret, melancholy, and curiosity. Only the roommate from Pakistan was in the room. He had already been there a couple of days and he served as my guide that day. Fortunately, my three years of night classes in English made it possible for me to manage but only today as I write this, do I realize how disorienting it must have been for my twelve-and-a-half-year-old brother who only knew a few English words. At four o'clock, a bell rang, and my roommate told me we needed to go for tea. We went down to the first floor into the dining hall. Three long tables occupied it, two in parallel and one the head table. The headmaster, the secretary, the lady my mother had rented a room from who was like a secretary-manager of the school, a couple of students, and the headmaster's ninety-year-old father sat at the head table. Three of the students poured tea in our cups. Making tea in Iran was an art in itself. Having the samovar at the correct temperature, letting the tea brew the precise amount of time, and poring it carefully in a cup was what made the tea so good. Now, my cup was filled with a very sweet chocolaty colored lukewarm liquid which tasted like a sweet cough syrup mixed with milk, one sip and a whisper in my ear by my roommate that you are not allowed to grimace like you are doing. A piece of cold toast and some jam were also served. I was glad when that half hour ended and going back to my room found my other two roommates who had just arrived. An Iranian and an Armenian from Tehran. My brother, on the other hand, was in a dorm room with ten other kids but a few weeks later was moved to a room with one student from Pakistan and two English boys.

The bell rang again at six pm. We went back to the dining hall for dinner. After grace by the headmaster, the students on duty for serving brought out our dinner: tomatoes on toast, canned tomatoes barely warmed on soggy toasted white bread. To drink, water or the mixture they called tea. The other secretary, who was a man in his early to mid-twenties, then came around to inspect that we ate it and started the process of humiliating us "foreigners" for our table manners. Since school did not officially begin till the next day, we had free time from seven to eight pm, and then we had to retire in our rooms.

As I mentioned earlier, my mother had accompanied us to Harrogate and rented a room across the street from the school. She wanted to make sure we were well settled and comfortable, but the school would not allow her to come and check our rooms. My dorm room must not have been larger than 12 by 10 feet at most, and it was shared by four of us, all foreigners. Two Iranian Armenians, One Iranian, and one Pakistani. No heat of course, just hot water bottles to keep warm at night.

I can write a lot about the experience at the school over the next two years, or nothing at all. I do think of it as, by and large, quite positive and helpful in moving me towards adulthood. I learned good table manners, how to be polite, to say, "yes sir or yes ma'am" and "no sir or no ma'am" in response to whatever was said to me, open the doors for the ladies and the elder, and study which I did, hard. I also learned to let the air of the hot water bottle before putting and closing the lid the hard way. There was a difference I noticed early with some surprise between how we related to our teachers at College Saint Louis and at Norwood College. At Saint Louis, we feared our teachers some but mostly respected them; at Norwood there was fear but a certain defiant casualness in the way students related, reacted, or spoke to the teachers even though always with "yes sir" "no sir." Frequently, they were made fun of behind their backs though the teachers were fully aware of the jokes. The headmaster, Charles Cass, was joked about as Charlie Cass is an Ass, and more than once I heard him mention this to say I know what you think about me, but not to prohibit such an attitude. I was also, especially in the beginning, very surprised—not to say shocked—by how much more sophisticated and nuanced was the way people thought and expressed themselves, especially our teachers in Tehran, compared with the almost crude nature of thinking I encountered at school. Additionally, pettiness, lying, goodie-two-shoesing were so prevalent at Norwood college, the kind of experience I had not had at College Saint Louis in Tehran. I did get used to it pretty fast however, and then I did not notice it anymore. I guess I became acclimated. There was, of course, prejudice against foreigners, and I remember how one time, having taken a geography test and passed with no errors, the teacher said that if he had graded me also on my English I would have failed. The same teacher once, thinking I was talking in class as opposed to the student sitting behind me, slapped me across the face. All the students encouraged me to report it to the headmaster who asked me whether the slap covered my ear or not. When I said I did not think so, he said then it is ok since most likely my ear drum was not damaged and there was no cause for a complaint. All good lessons to learn in life especially when you were raised feeling very much protected by your parents. The England of the sixties was a bit of a bigoted place. Either you were British, or you were a foreigner and therefore of secondary status. In Yorkshire, where the school was, anything across the waters, English Channel, or Atlantic ocean was not English and therefore inferior. I explained it to myself as an oddity of the British people because, in terms of the standard of living and the primitive nature of home facilities, it seemed they were inferior to what I was used to in Tehran. And, as I have said, I did not find their thinking as sophisticated as the Iranians and the French I had interacted with in Tehran.

After learning that the English way of education had important differences to my prior French education, and learning to correct for it especially in response to being humiliated a few times by teachers and the headmaster, I must have felt a sense of "I'll show you," and worked very hard, more than any other student in the school, at least in terms of the number of hours I spent studying and, therefore, I did well and was able to pass my General Certificate of Education, O'level exams, and enter "The Leeds College of Technology" in the nearby city of Leeds. On the wise suggestion of the headmaster who offered me my own room at the school, I remained at the boarding school another year, commuting by train or bus to Leeds every day and then, the following year, summer of 1962, moved to Leeds and rented an apartment with other Iranian friends. My life in Leeds, once I moved there, was going to classes, studying, and over a relatively short period of time, going out to pubs and discotheques. Soon, girls became part of my life. English girls, at least those I met, were quite forward, and some, even though younger, were a lot more daring and physical. Necking in the movie theatres was the main activity, and by the middle of that year I had a full-time girlfriend, and the following year rented the first floor of a house, and she moved in with me. She was a year and a half older, much more experienced, but her parents were not happy especially because I was not English and not Jewish.

After two years in Leeds, during which I had my first and second car and travelled numerous times to various parts of England, including to Liverpool for football, and became a bit of a bettor, betting on horse races and dog races, I passed my A'level GCEs in mainly science subjects and, by the beginning of 1964, began thinking of medical schools.

In thinking back about those years and my teachers, only three had an impact on me. The headmaster of the boarding school was not one of them. The science teacher and the French teacher at Norwood College, and the Zoology teacher at Leeds College. The science teacher because he was very matter of fact but fair and showed no prejudice, and he made sure you thoroughly understood anything he taught, the zoology teacher because he seemed to genuinely care about my education beyond just his subject, and the French teacher who also genuinely cared about me and my future. In fact, even when in Leeds I continued to take French with him privately, and so I had a relationship with him for four years. He even invited me to his house in Bradford for tea with his wife. I always remember what he said to me when I expressed anxiety, asking about "What if I don't pass my A'levels and therefore not be able to start medical school for another year, and was I wasting my time?" He said increasing knowledge by studying another year is never a waste of time. What you learn stays with you for life.

I had no guidance and applied to and explored schools in London and Paris. When I reported what I was doing to my father, he suggested, on the advice of a friend of his, that I should check the "Catholique University of Louvain" (Leuven) in Belgium. I went to Louvain and walked to the administrative building of the medical school and spoke to the secretary. She told me who to go see—one of the professors in charge of admission—which I did, and after a brief interview, he told me I could start in September and skip the first year. In Belgium and many European countries at the time, medical school was 7 years of which the seventh year was the internship year. With the offer of skipping the first year, I stopped my search and chose Louvain over the Sorbonne in Paris and Middlesex Hospital in London, and went to Tehran for the summer and began medical school that Fall. The trip to Tehran made me realize that when you are not there with your friends all the time, their lives move on, and when you come back, there is not the same place for you as there was before. In some way I felt a bit like an outsider, and this helped diminish my occasional nostalgia about the past. Things had changed.

I arrived in Louvain a few days before the start of the academic year and rented a hotel room. I knew no one, and I had to find my way around where to go, where to get the books I was going to need, and then find out the schedule of the classes and their location, and then find the addresses. It took a few days to begin to find some ease in orienting myself, and then I began the classes. Very quickly I heard a few students speak English and found out they were Americans. We quickly became friends and their know-how about where to live helped me leave the hotel and rent a room in a building owned by the university for its students. I was on the third floor and there was an American from New Jersey, another from New York on my floor, as well as a Canadian. Life was going to class, studying, studying, studying, and then going out for food and maybe a couple of beers, and on the weekends to the one discotheque in town. Later that Fall, my father bought me an Alfa Romeo 2600 Spider which allowed me, and some of my friends, to explore Brussels, Antwerp, and other smaller towns.

I was in Medical school about six months when I met a Belgian Flemish girl, and a year later, we were married. She came from a family of 5 children: her older brother, her identical twin sister, and two younger brothers. Her mother was a nurse who had given up nursing to be with the children, and her father was a doctor. I got along well with her parents, and her father was a major influence on me in the way I saw medicine and the doctor's role. I did well at school, especially after I got married. Life was enjoyable, I had a sense of family again and a little over a year into the marriage we had our first child Caroline. The delivery was difficult and Caroline weighed less than six pounds.

I have often said that I never liked school until the beginning of clinical years at Louvain. The first three years being essentially, though not only, basic sciences, the study of diseases, their diagnosis, and etiology; treatment does not begin till the fourth year, called *"premier doctorat."* I loved the three doctorate years and enjoyed almost everything. I also studied very hard and received a distinction the first doctorate year, and Magna Cum Laude the subsequent years, and graduated Magna Cum Laude. It seemed to me for the first time that what I was learning was in fact useful. Not only interesting, eye opening, and mystery-solving, but that actually I could one day use this knowledge, and that for now I could actually understand my Diphtheria, Scarlet Fever, and other diseases I had contracted as a child but, most importantly, understand Typhoid Fever which had brought me very close to death. To this day, as I am writing these pages, I cannot imagine for me a more interesting subject than medicine.

In the beginning of the sixth year, through my American friends, I discovered that I could do the seventh year in Canada and have a real internship, as opposed to Louvain where you were not allowed to do much as an intern. I was lucky to be accepted at the Hotel Dieu de Montreal, and in June 1969 I began my rotating internship.

I remember arriving in Montreal alone with a plan to rent an apartment within a day or so of my arrival, thinking the hospital administrator would have suggestions. Little did I know that I arrived on "Saint Jean Baptiste Day," a big holiday in Quebec, and also the occasion of a huge demonstration with some violence of the separatist movement. Ironical, because I had just spent a few years in another country with frequent demonstrations, this time to separate Flanders from Wallonie. Louvain, was in Flemish country, and there was a constant demand for the French part of the university to leave it. In fact, a couple years after I graduated it did, "Louvain la Neuve" was created near Brussels, and the French university left Leuven which now only had the "Catholieke Universiteit Leuven." In the years I was in Leuven, it was a small university town and very pleasant since the majority of the population were students, I visited it many years later and, like most places, it was no longer the same, as many industries and a much-expanded brewery had moved into all the surrounding country side.

Back to Montreal, I realized that first day that I needed to stay in a hotel and look for an apartment the next day. A starting intern like myself, I met when I checked in the hospital that first day, was nice enough to take me to where she lived and see if they had other space to rent, which they did not. She then took me to a recently finished apartment complex not too far from the hospital where I was able to rent a one-bedroom apartment and moved in the next day, sleeping on a mattress the concierge lent me until I was able to buy a bed and then the furniture, and then my car, which we had shipped from Belgium, arrived. Caroline and her mother only came once everything was settled. By then, my life as a doctor and a bread-winner had started, and I was even enjoying the "all night" calls which would end with me coming home early in the morning and, despite the early hour, finding Caroline awake sitting in the living room waiting for me so together we could watch her favorite TV cartoons while her mother was sleeping.

CHAPTER 3

Beginning Work Life

Finally, after all those years of studying and learning, I was going to continue learning but also earning. The internship salary was around $4600 a year which seemed hugely above zero.

My first rotation was psychiatry. I was told my first day I was on call and that calls started at 5 pm. So, I did not go to the hospital till that afternoon, to find out they had been looking for me because I was to start work that morning and be on call after the regular work day. I knew so little that I had assumed if I am on call then I don't work that day. I also did not know being on call meant I also covered the emergency room, so with rudimentary knowledge on that first day, I suddenly had to deal with acute psychotic patients brought to the ER and prescribe psychotropic medications which I had never done before. My first prescription was a small dose of Valium or Librium, I don't recall which, to a female patient brought in to the emergency room by relatives and police. The nurse asked me if that was all I was prescribing and I said yes, it is a strong medication. I was called back to the patient's room a short time later to find she had thrown everything around and had bent the metal table on top of her bed. She was a bipolar patient in a manic phase, and I learnt my first lesson.

My first contact with psychiatry and mental illness was through a course in medical school. It was a traditional course, using significant amount of Kraepelinian classification of mental illness. It was totally uninteresting to me, and consequently the two months in the psychiatry rotation in Montreal were not particularly gratifying. I did, however, enjoy the twice-weekly hour-long classes given by two psychoanalysts. Psychiatry seemed to me not more than making one of a handful of diagnoses and prescribing medication. Psychoanalysis, on the other hand, provided a road map to understand many conditions and to understand people. Also, given my interest in mystery, it could give me the tools to discover that which was unknown, in the unconscious. In medical school I had very much enjoyed a course we had on medical psychology given by a psychoanalyst, Professor Mertens de Wilmars, who essentially taught us Karl Abraham's Theory of Psychopathology. With this course, I felt I could understand the reasons for the presence of symptoms and therefore be able to help the patient overcome his or her symptoms through this understanding. Since the course relied heavily on the clear classification of mental conditions and the causative factors, it was quite seductive for someone interested in problem-solving. Today, of course, I would say Abraham's classification is not only without much scientific merit, but is both simplistic and concrete. I will review his ideas later, but suffice it to say here that for me, as a young medical student, it elicited the same sense of awe and understanding that immunology or etiology of diseases had. To know what a condition was caused by, and how the cause could explain all the manifestations was a most pleasurable insight There was another reason for my interest in psychoanalytic thinking, and it was stimulated by a book by Michael Balint entitled *The Doctor, His Patient and the Illness.* This was about how medical doctors sometimes missed diagnosing their patients due to a lack of listening and figuring out what was happening in the patient's life. It seemed to me that as a psychoanalyst I would discover causes of illness which were missed by the other medical specialists. A book called *An Elementary Textbook of Psychoanalysis* by Charles Brenner, who became a supervisor, and then a friend, many years later, also stimulated my interest in psychoanalysis.

However, in medical school, my interests remained on internal medicine because of the focus on diagnosis and immunology, because it was new, and because it was contributing to all kinds of discoveries and ways of conceptualizing disease.

I was happy to end my rotation in psychiatry, and I wished it had been shorter.

Obstetrics and Gynecology followed Psychiatry, and though it was tough because of the hours, it was a great education. It gave me a lot of self-confidence and a feeling that problems will inevitably come up, but they can be handled. Delivering two, three, or more babies a day, and assisting C-sections during a two-month rotation helped me to fully assume the role of a doctor. It was also the first time I made a little money on the side. One of the attending obstetricians did not like to come to the hospital until the last minute, so if you would stay in regular telephone contact with him until his patient had sufficient cervical dilation to expect birth soon, he would give you five dollars after you assisted him in the delivery. At the hospital where I did my OB/GYN rotation, most patients were of limited means, or were unwed mothers, and interns delivered their babies; attendings delivered their private patients; and residents mostly dealt with complicated cases or assisting gynecological surgery.

Pediatrics followed and I realized it was not for me; I think of all the rotations, pediatrics made me the most nervous. Firstly, the majority of patients do not speak yet and those who speak cannot yet fully describe what is ailing them, and for some reason it seemed to me that making a mistake in pediatrics would be horrifying. I did have one highly anxious moment while in the pediatric emergency room, I decided that a young patient needed a spinal tap to rule out meningitis. I asked the resident if I could do the tap and he, after a little hesitation, agreed. The way it works is that you have a needle that is in two parts: the needle, and a part like a small tubule. After you push the needle into the space between the vertebrae, you remove the actual needle and collect the fluid that comes out of the tubule, and then quickly place the needle back to prevent excessive leakage of spinal fluid.

Everything went well until after I had removed the needle, left the hollow part in and allowed the pressured liquid to fly out, but when I had to quickly put the needle back in to prevent more liquid than was needed to squirt out the child began moving, my hand began shaking and more spinal fluid squirted out, and it took me what seemed like eternity (and which was perhaps no more than fifteen seconds), before I was able to push the needle back in through the small hole. This was a particularly frightening moment as had more spinal fluid squirted out, it could have caused a herniation of the lower part of the brain and killed the patient. As I wrote the above, I found my level of anxiety was highest in pediatrics.

Internal medicine, which was mostly in endocrinology and cardiology, except when on call—at which point you were responsible for all types of cases—followed. I saw a lot, including a man in his early thirties coming at 2.00 am to the ER with two women in their twenties, to get tested for venereal disease, or people coming in to have a physical at hours well past midnight because they were going on vacation or moving the next day.

I saw a lot of challenging cases also: ventricular tachycardia, infarcts, intestinal obstructions, fractures, facial injuries from fist fights, and so on. Two cases remain on my mind because of the sadness attached to them. One, a young woman about whom the nurse whispered in my ear was the most famous erotic film star in Quebec, consulting for vaginal bleeding, thinking perhaps she was miscarrying. The physical examination revealed petechiae all over her body which meant something systemic was going on, and the hematologist I called hospitalized her and told me the next day that it was most likely leukemia. Another sad story was a middle-aged woman brought in with symptoms of confusion and a history of being diagnosed as suffering from hysteria. Unfortunately, on neurological examination I found a positive Babinski, called the neurosurgery resident on call. She had a head X-ray and was taken to the O.R. shortly afterwards with a strong suspicion of a Glioblastoma. What pains me to this day, aside from the sad prognosis for this young person, is that after she was taken from the ER, I totally forgot her husband who had brought her in, who had told me about the history of hysteria, and who was in the waiting room. Only when, at 6.00 pm or so, some three hours later, I walked through the waiting room to go to the cafeteria and saw him just sitting there waiting with no idea of what was happening upstairs in the O.R. did I realize my negligence. I think of my lapse in this situation often and always with self-reproach.

Fortunately, most cases that came to the ER were treatable, and though some needed to be hospitalized, they did not have life-threatening conditions.

Surgery followed medicine. It meant being in the O.R. a good part of the day, and when on call every third day, being in the E.R. all night. I learnt a good deal assisting the surgeon and the residents in surgery, but I did not really enjoy it. For an intern, assisting meant standing next to the resident with the surgeon on the other side, and retracting—that is to say keeping the incision open and moving the organs not concerned in the surgery out of the way. Some surgeons worked efficiently and quickly, and some obsessed, and then there were those who ran an experiment during the surgical intervention. Some had to do with changes of technique, and some had to do with taking certain measurements which would prove this or that pet theory of the surgeon. In those situations, a procedure that would take normally two-and-a-half hours, could take four or more hours.

I still remember the first time I walked into an operating room. It was not during my rotation in surgery but in gynecology. I washed my hands as I was told, which is a procedure in itself due to the danger of carrying an infection into the O.R., and walked in to get the surgical garb put on me, and the surgeon said "No, no, go out, and wash your hands." He did these three times until I realized, from the nurse whispering in my ear, that when I walked in to be dressed in surgical garb, I let my hands fall below my belt line, thus creating a danger of contamination.

While I did not particularly like assisting which meant retracting the incision to keep it open for the surgeon for long hours in the O.R., I liked surgical outpatient, especially because the chief resident, who was Belgian and had become a friend, would teach me and then let me subsequently do many outpatient type procedures. I became so big-headed in the process, that one time, a patient was brought in to the E.R. with repeated vomiting. I diagnosed an obstruction and, without consulting the resident, introduced a gastric tube—the first time ever for me. The procedure went fine, but when the resident and attending arrived, they called me to say that I did something that was not needed and could have been dangerous. I was lucky they did not initiate a disciplinary action.

During the time I was in surgery, I also met residents who did not have interns under them, specialties like ear, nose and throat, ophthalmology, and orthopedics. Very quickly, a few of them offered me six dollars for a pre-surgery physical. They did not want to do it themselves, and so I took care of it. Sometimes I would have six or more pre-op physicals to do, naturally in addition to my own pre-op patients mostly being operated for abdominal surgeries: gall bladder, stomach, intestines (mostly colon), kidneys, hernias, and hemorrhoids. I accepted these extra jobs not only because they gave a few extra dollars to do things with, such as presents for my daughter, but also, I enjoyed the confidence they had in me, and my clinical judgment. One cannot overlook anything prior to surgery because sometimes the cost can be great; like, for example, patients who go into delirium tremens after an operation because the physicians did not enquire about alcohol use and abuse.

My final month in surgical rotation was in neurosurgery, which I continued to think about as a choice of career for me. The department had five or six neurosurgeons but only one fellow. A fellow is someone who has done a surgical residency and is now specializing in neurosurgery. The poor guy was on call every day, and you could see the exhaustion on his face; he was a very nice guy and kept doing his best despite the pressure. Because of this, most neurological surgeries had just the attending and the intern, in this case me, since I was the only intern who had requested a neurosurgery rotation. I very quickly was taught how to suture the incisions, and the surgeons would leave me to close them up. I loved doing it, and slowly did more of it, including not just the skin layers but also the muscles. I should clarify that these were mostly, if not all, back surgeries for sciatic hernias. During the whole time in neurosurgery, I assisted surgery that was not back-related only half a dozen times, and one time, which was new then, microscopic brain surgery. The surgeon doing the microscopic surgery was the youngest member of the neurosurgical team and actively encouraged me to apply for the residency and fellowship, and offered to support my application but, at the end, relying on my experience that most of neurosurgery was back surgery, I decided to definitely do psychiatry in order to become a psychoanalyst.

If there is any time of my life that I would happily relive, or if possible go back to, it would be the year as a rotating intern. To this day, I cannot imagine a more gratifying and interesting area of study than medicine.

My wife's sister and her family lived in New York and, prior to starting the neurosurgery rotation, we had visited them briefly and I had arranged an interview at a psychiatric training program at Hillside Hospital. The program was recommended to me by one of the psychoanalyst teachers in Montreal as a psychoanalytically oriented training program. My interviews went well, and I was offered a position, so when I finally made up my mind to do psychiatry, after finishing my neurosurgery rotation, at the end of June 1970, I moved to Glen Oaks, New York.

I had not given too much thought to being accepted for training at such a late date, but soon found out it was because Hillside had agreed to cover the psychiatric wing of Queens General Hospital, a New York City Public Hospital. As a result, they needed more residents, and they chose to send the four residents who were foreign graduates to Queens Hospital, and to keep the American Medical School graduates at Hillside. So, while living in Hillside housing behind that hospital, I had to travel to Queens Hospital a good 20 minutes away, depending on traffic. For a hospital, Hillside was luxurious: beautiful grounds, nice cafeteria, beautiful meeting rooms, and private offices for the residents. Obviously, this was not the case in Queens Hospital, and at first I was a bit taken aback at not being told upfront about the assignment, but as time went on, and now years after, I realize how much better an experience it was. Hillside was for long-term hospitalization; Queens Hospital was much more for acute care and therefore the volume and variety of cases was much greater and the learning potential much richer. The facilities were ordinary if not a bit in shambles, and we even avoided the cafeteria by buying lunch in nearby Delicatessens, but you encountered patients suffering from a wide array of disorders in the emergency room and the hospitalized patients needed much more active management. Now, all these years later, I remain convinced that I ended up having a better experience than if I had spent the first year at Hillside Hospital itself. I realize I am at risk of being seen as bragging, but I became well regarded by the attending and nursing staff at Queens, and then at Hillside, and was even asked, over more senior residents, to take over running the lecture program at Hillside and invite prominent psychiatrists and psychoanalysts to speak to the staff.

The second year at Hillside is most memorable however, for the birth of my second child, this time a boy whom we named Gregory Khachatour after my half brother Grigor, and my father. From early on, he was very easygoing and cheerful, and I distributed cigars to my colleagues as was the custom in those days. My daughter by then was five, very close to me, and attending a local kindergarten a very short walking distance from the hospital.

During this second year of training, again, what had happened before happened again: two residents asked me to take the night call in their place for 20 dollars a night, which I accepted. The reason for their not wanting to do night call was anxiety of not knowing how to deal with the emergencies that occasionally came up, such as patients who needed to be sutured because they had tried to slash their wrists, or older patients with physical ailments that needed to be monitored, for example, developing pulmonary edema, or having medication side-effects. The administration found out about this after it had been going on for a month or so, but the two residents managed to convince them not to prevent it.

My family life during this time was okay; I had always been crazy about my daughter, and now I was also crazy about my son. We saw my sister-in-law and her family regularly. My brother-in-law was already quite successful, and we would spend weekends in their large house and go on their motorboat on the Hudson River.

My marriage was only okay retrospectively. At the time it seemed fine, it was what I knew, and I tolerated and tried to be supportive of my wife's occasional unexplainable irritable moods, as well as bouts of brief, three- or four-day depressions. They were there from the beginning of our marriage, and, along with her occasional absences for hours longer than anticipated on certain days, things were okay. Finally, in the summer of 1974, I decided to end the marriage. It was a very difficult time for me and yet I felt I had no other choice, and my analyst, with whom I started in 1972, encouraged me to end it.

It was during the second year of my residency that I applied for psychoanalytic training. At the time the American Psychoanalytic Association required at least two years of psychiatric residency prior to becoming eligible for psychoanalytic training. The two most prestigious institutes at that time were The New York Psychoanalytic Institute and Society, and the Downstate Psychoanalytic institute. Many of the teachers at Hillside were from Downstate. I applied to both. It was not easy in those days—the golden days—to be accepted into psychoanalytic institutes like

New York and Downstate. The interviewing process was very extensive. I had three interviewers for New York, and was interviewed for a total of eight hours. For Downstate, I had two interviewers and was interviewed for about five hours. I was accepted to both in early May. The institutes had an agreement to notify all applicants on the same day in early May. Then came time for me to decide which one to accept. I liked my psychoanalyst teachers at Downstate, and the people I asked were of the opinion that both were excellent and that I could not make a mistake, whichever one I chose. Then, sitting at lunch with other residents and two attendings from the units, including my unit chief, I was asked if I had decided, and one of the people around the table said, "Well, New York has more prestige," to which my unit chief said, "Prestige never hurts," so, I chose the New York Psychoanalytic Institute.

Soon after sending my letter of acceptance, I was given the name of a psychoanalyst to consult, who, if he agreed, would be my doctor. He was located on Park Avenue and 92nd Street. It occurred to me suddenly that this meant I had to commute five-times-a-week to Manhattan. This appeared like a tough obstacle to surmount. Therefore, I quickly made some inquiries about other residency programs, and called the Payne Whitney Clinic of New York Hospital to see if they would consider an application. The secretary of the director of training called me back and gave me an appointment to meet with the director. I went to Payne Whitney, met with him; he then arranged for me to meet another member of the department and, within days, informed me that I was accepted, and asked me to come and meet with the secretary of the Chairman who would discuss housing. I met her, was assigned a two-bedroom apartment on the 23rd floor of the building across the street from the Cornell Medical School, and she even agreed to arrange for a parking spot in the hospital garage—which was well worth my gift of a bottle of Chanel No. 5.

On June 30, 1972, my family moved to Manhattan. By then I had had my two appointments with my future psychoanalyst, and had scheduled our appointments (five times per week) to begin in September.

I realize that I have moved rather quickly through a significant number of years and experiences, and have only given a very limited picture, leaving out all the meaningful experiences, whether of joy or sadness and pain, success or failure, whether full of anxiety or pleasurable. I have done so because I consider this book to be about the evolution of psychoanalysis and the end of Freud which render the details of my personal life irrelevant.

Nevertheless, since coming to the end of these first chapters some time ago, I have been preoccupied, and have ruminated about whether I did not gloss too quickly over my formative years. What I wrote is obviously very condensed, but I think is as accurate as any narrative about one's life can be, perhaps I could do a better job of describing how I experienced life in those periods, that is from the time I left Tehran, to the time I began at the New York Psychoanalytic Institute. The town of Harrogate, its unfamiliar streets becoming familiar, the park near the school where I passed through every day to get the train to Leeds in my second year, the beautiful spring and the dreary winters, the smells, learning about "a pint of bitter," the sense of discovery, not only of places but of people, of character, of generosity and pettiness, the pleasures and the dreads, the sense of independence when I moved to Leeds, the big city, learning my way around, hearing the Beatles song "Love Me Do," and thinking it inferior to Elvis Presley's release of "It's Now or Never" in 1963—There are details, and details, and details, but while they may be, at least some of them, important to me, they may be boring to whoever reads these words. I am also mindful that Freud, some, and Ernst Kris to a greater degree, and many other psychoanalysts, have written about the inaccuracies of memory and, over the last few decades, neuropsychologists and scientists have further elaborated and proven the ubiquitous nature of autobiographic memory distortion. So, for now, all I want to say is that what I have written is what I remember relatively with ease, but have no way of corroborating its complete accuracy or lack thereof anymore. Am I excluding more difficult recollections? Do the ones I write about hide other stories? Are aspects of my inner life, fantasies, wishes pushed aside? In truth, I do not know the answer, and also, since I am not a real writer, even if I had access to them, it would be hard for me to create a cohesive life story. However, I do know that everything I have experienced in my life, from day one, has made me who I am, and that may be glanced at from these notes. Perhaps, if I were in touch with friends in England, Belgium, and Montreal, or my residency days in New York, I could recollect more, stimulated by their recollections, but for now, only my brother who was with me in Harrogate, and then in Leeds, and briefly in Louvain, is a source, and we do share stories when we see each other, but to myself I often remark how our memories and our experiences of shared moments are different. Similar in a broad way, but very different in detail, and even in our subjective sense.

Suffice it to say that when I look over my life, I have two sets of realities, if that is the correct word. One set is made up of a series of memories that hang together and create a narrative, a life history or story which I have described in a cursory manner, in the sense that I remember more but don't feel the additional memories would add much to the narrative I have revealed. But there is another reality which seems to be less real or not as concretely defined, which is life as lived and not as easily remembered within a narrative. It is this second group, a more elusive reality, full of questions and ambiguities that better defines who I am, where I am in my life, and how I got here. But what did I experience, and what did I forget?

In this second reality I also come face to face with aspects of my character that I only know about because I am told, but I don't actually see, or more tellingly, I don't feel. Psychoanalysis is primarily about this aspect, what the analysand does not see, and yet is central to who she or he is, and that determines much of the relationships, achievements, failures and the un-understandable reactions in daily life. In my case, I also do not see the expression of certain feelings or intentions of others towards me, and I am frequently surprised when someone points them out to me. I don't know why this is so, and I am myself surprised when suddenly I realize, sometimes years later, that this is what the other person was after. There is one possible determinant for this and, unfortunately, it was never really dealt with in my personal analysis. When I was in Louvain, my brother moved there too, and began work as an intern for an engineering design company.

Soon after, his English girlfriend moved in with him. Her parents, however, put in a condition that they would only allow that if my mother were there, and so my mother came and lived with them until they got married when he was seventeen-and-a-half years old. One night, my brother and his girlfriend had gone out, and my mother invited me to have dinner with her, and made some delicious Persian dish. That night, as she was anticipating my brother's upcoming wedding, and therefore her ability to return to Tehran, with tears in her eyes she told me that my father's left eye was a glass eye. I had never known this until that moment. Did I not notice it? Did I deny it? Did I make myself blind to it? I don't know, but could it have contributed to that aspect of my character I described above? Perhaps.

Before I end this chapter, since I have presented a narrative of my life made up of my memories, I will briefly mention one of my differences with Freudian theory which will become clearer as I move on in this work. For Freud, recollection of traumatic memories was key to the therapeutic success. During his life and long after, to some extent to this day, the idea of repressed memories, and the unearthing of them for therapeutic purposes, has been a central tenet of psychoanalysis. He asserted that when a wish of a forbidden nature is aroused in a specific moment, then that impulse and the circumstances arousing it, i.e., the memory of the event, are repressed, and this leads to the formation of symptoms and even character. What I have described above, namely the distinction between the narrative of one's life vs. life as lived and experienced, presents a different perspective from Freud's. For one to understand someone, you need to understand, as much as possible, what they have experienced and how the experiences have contributed to them being who they are. Individual memories, distorted as they are, provide us some clues to the nature of the experiences and accompanying emotions, but. in of themselves, they do not lead to change. Restoring a repressed memory may offer us a clue to the type of life that may have led to the repression (which I will discuss later) but not much more. Understanding, over a period of time, the life a person has had is what constitutes for me the path of psychoanalysis. But more about this later. I will just briefly say here that it seems to me rather self-evident that a memory of an event and—to stay within Freudian theory—of a traumatic event, does not in any way tell the whole story. The event affects the person in many ways and alters the way they see and understand or don't understand things, and this affects the next related event, and gradually affects their way of being.

CHAPTER 4

The New York Psychoanalytic Institute and Society

On September 11, 1972, at 8.00 pm, I finished seeing my last patient of the day and walked over from my office at 823 Park Avenue between 75th and 76th streets to the New York Psychoanalytic Institute. On the way I bought an oatmeal raisin cookie to keep me going until dinner at home at 10:15 or so. It was going to be my first passage through the heavy doors into a path that would determine my professional journey. I did not, at the time, think that I would go through those doors some two or three thousand more times. In fact, my plan was to do psychoanalytic training and then go back to Belgium. I had already applied for citizenship in Belgium, and was awaiting the progress of further administrative steps before obtaining it. Little did I know or think that once you commit to psychoanalytic work, your ability to pick up and leave to another town, let alone another country, becomes close to impossible, certainly quite unfeasible. Instead, my life over the years became totally centered on the Institute—something I never had imagined. When I had been fascinated by psychoanalytic theory in Louvain, and later a bit more in Montreal, I did not appreciate what it involved, but soon I understood. Three nights a week classes from 8.30 to 10.00pm; 5 times a week personal analysis; two very low-fee patients ($1 and $2); and then 1 hour of supervision for each patient until obtaining permission to have one case unsupervised. Most importantly, however, it was a commitment to an ongoing intense intellectual activity, mostly centered at the institute, until retirement.

But, isn't it always so? When you are starting your adult life, you look at the road ahead, yes, occasionally you think back, but the majority of the time is looking ahead, fulfilling ambitions, desires, even fantasies. You know your actions have consequences, but you don't fully appreciate those consequences. You think of marriage, children, buying a home. Then children's schooling, maybe buying a weekend home, going on vacation. You focus on your work, on your patients, your life at the institute, your ambitions at the institute, becoming a teacher, a training analyst, and you go through days, weeks, months, years looking ahead and then you come to a point that what is left of your life gets shorter and shorter. This is when you look back. You think of your choices, your decisions, the good times, the hardships. You are on the same highway, but the feelings are different and the thoughts follow them. So, yes, when I walked through those doors in 1972, I did not fully appreciate what train I was taking.

In thinking about the highway, I have begun to see things a bit differently. I have begun to wonder if we don't recognize that while there is a continuity in life, there is also a kind of discontinuity. This has become more evident to me as I have been a grandfather now. I have realized that, in fact, we don't have one life but many. I can almost say a part of us dies, and a new part takes over. I look at my five-year-old granddaughter and I know, based on seeing my eighteen-year-old-grandson grow up, that when she is 10 she will be very very different than how she is now, and when fifteen, very different from both. So, I have begun to think that despite the thread that connects life, we keep dying—meaning no longer existing in the previous way of being—and we do this until our last day. We don't have one state of being with its own fantasies, emotions, thoughts and processes, but many such states. There is a continuity in the sense that the various stages or times effect the following ones but, nevertheless, they do cease to exist in an observational and experiential manner. Freud believed that the three-year- or five-year- or eight-year-old existed in us, and I think yes and no. Time, events, relationships, and the addition of years changes us, and sometimes to a higher degree than Freud assumed. To state it in Freudian language, let us say oedipal conflicts may be prominent at five or ten years of age (that is if they were as Freud described them) but it does not mean they will have any role to play in our lives and who we are when we are thirty. Each period of our life dies and is replaced while, nevertheless, a thread made up of our genes and prior experiences persists.

Now, to give a sense of psychoanalytic training, scholarship, and commitment, I would like to take us back forty-nine years, and describe what things were like then. I use. the vague term "things" because I cannot find a term that describes the state of theory, the social climate, the sense of certainty, the sense of awe and continuing discovery, the dismissal of other views, the infighting, the arrogance, the prestige and more. I hope, not too clumsily, to review where psychoanalysis was back then.

In 1972, mental conditions were basically divided into four major groups: the neurosis; the psychosis; the character disorders, and the perversions. All of neurosis, character disorders and perversions were considered to be treatable by psychoanalysis. Yes, there was behavior therapy and hypnosis still a bit, but psychoanalysis and psychoanalytically oriented psychotherapy were the choice treatments. Then there were the psychoses, the many clinical groupings of schizophrenia, and the manic disorders, along with melancholia and severe forms of depression. The classification of types of schizophrenia and its symptomatology were based on the works of the Swiss psychiatrist, Eugene Bleuler and Kraepelin and his descriptions and classifications were discarded. By 1972, most psychiatrist considered medication with psychotherapy, based on psychoanalytic theory (what was also called insight-oriented therapy) as the treatment of choice for the psychoses, and psychoanalysis the treatment of choice, when feasible, for the other conditions. The brain was basically ignored in all psychiatric conditions despite the use of medication. It was all in the mind, and psychoanalytic theory was the theory of the mind. At Hillside hospital where I began my training, the medical director was a Meninger-clinic trained psychoanalyst (Meninger was considered one of the best psychiatric hospitals at the time, and very psychoanalytically oriented), and the training director was a psychoanalyst. Though not all the unit chiefs and outpatient department staff were psychoanalysts, many were very psychoanalytically oriented, and thought us psychotherapy based on Freudian theory. There was one major exception, and this was the person who can fairly be considered one of the fathers of psychopharmacologic treatment in the US. Donald Klein was head of research, and he had two other psychiatrists on his team, and they were the people we consulted whenever we had more complex medication questions. Klein taught the pharmacology course in the second year of residency, and I remember him saying that obsessive-compulsive disorder was more prevalent in an Eastern European country—which meant to him that it could be inherited and was therefore a brain disorder. Many of us laughed at this and another idea about depression being a brain disease because sometimes certain foods, particularly chocolate, would improve the persons mood. We thought these were crazy ideas because there was no doubt in our minds at the time, 1972, that these were diseases caused by psychic conflict, as Freud had described them in a number of papers on obsessive-compulsive neurosis, such as the cases of the "The Rat man" and the "Wolf Man," and in his seminal paper for depression: "Mourning and Melancholia." Donald Klein was also very focused on the nuances of diagnosis and, not infrequently, he would disagree with the other clinicians on the phenomenology. He liked precision. I still have a letter from him, produced here, from Dec. 14. 1971.

THE NEW YORK PSYCHOANALYTIC INSTITUTE AND SOCIETY

HILLSIDE HOSPITAL

INTER-OFFICE MEMORANDUM

HH FORM NO. 123

TO: Dr. Nersessian

FROM: Dr. Klein

DATE: 12/14/71

SUBJECT:

I am sorry that I did not have a chance to discuss with you, following the last initial conference, the question of the VonDomarus principle and its relationship to psychotic thinking.

Briefly, predicate identification or paleologic is attributed... to schizophrenics who are supposed to follow the deductive model "a is b, c is b, therefore a is c." I don't believe this at all and further, studies of syllogistic reasoning in schizophrenics have never shown them to be prone to this sort of illogic.

Also, the example given by you of your patient's thought disorder did not follow the predicate identification model but rather the premise justification model.

The patient said "I am the devil. I am born under the sign of Aquarius" and therefore drew the logical conclusion that the devil was born under the sign of Aquarius. He needed to maintain this or otherwise he could not be the devil.

The situation did not obtain that he learned on some external source that the devil was born under Aquarius, realized that he also was an Aquarius, and therefore, concluded that he was the devil; which would have been the sort of logic that predicate identification would demand.

I view the flaw in psychotic thinking as a disorder of induction rather than deduction and suggest that you review the section in my book on psychosis, in particular, pages 33 to 40.

DFK:qp

Aside from exceptions like Klein and a number of others, American psychiatry was essentially Freudian, as were many of the chairmen of departments. Cornell University was an exception until 1974 when a psychoanalyst, Robert Michels, became the Chairman of the department.

To someone in psychiatric training, it therefore seemed that if it could be afforded, the path forward after the residency in psychiatry was to become a psychoanalyst, and if not, to try to have as much supervision as possible with psychoanalyst supervisors to learn how to do psychoanalytic psychotherapy. Of course, psychoanalytic views permeated, and sometimes dominated, other fields of study: history, literature, philosophy, art, anthropology, and even cinema. Given this situation, being a psychoanalysts had a certain cache and lay persons often expressed a great deal of curiosity about it.

Anyhow, in the early seventies psychoanalysis was at its heights, perhaps slightly less so than in the fifties or sixties, but still pretty high. I was a total believer, and. at New York Psychoanalytic, Freud was the leader, and it is where I began my journey.

The New York Psychoanalytic Institute and Society is located on East 82nd street, close to Second Avenue in Manhattan. The building is four stories high, and about thirty feet wide, and has a finished basement. It is a relatively attractive building which would have stood out better in a more prestigious neighborhood, and have been more in synchrony with the reputation of the place. The entrance door is made of wood and is heavy, as if to symbolize how hard it is or at least was in 1972 to get into the place, but also it gave one a sense of being closed off from the mundane, comings . and goings, of Second Avenue. When I first opened the door, with a palpable sense of trepidation, I was taken aback by the old-fashioned and shabby interior. It looked as if nothing had been done to it for a long time, perhaps from when it was actually purchased some decades earlier. The main presence on the entrance floor was and is the library, probably the most extensive and well stocked psychoanalytic library in the world, including a rich archive. There was a head librarian and two other librarians who supplied us with reading materials and told us which classroom to go to. The Place functioned very efficiently.

The mood inside the building can best be described as very serious. Freud had, in his technical recommendations for therapeutic analysis, that the psychoanalyst maintain anonymity. What this meant in practical terms is that he or she did not divulge any information about himself, and did not discuss his preferences, likes or dislikes of everyday life. This attitude was, at NYPSI, applied to all interactions. The teachers did not reveal or discuss anything about themselves, and maintained a serious and somewhat distant demeanor in their interactions with us, similar to our personal psychoanalysts. As an extension of this posture, all staff did the same. This contributed further to the sense that rules of social interaction were different once inside the building. Over time, and certainly by the last year, this "keeping at a distance" significantly diminished, and our relationship with our teachers became somewhat more open. Nonetheless the whole atmosphere at the institute in the early years contributed to a feeling of uniqueness and specialness, amplified by the broader perception of NYPSI as the Mecca of psychoanalysis.

The schedule was taxing; we, the students, all worked in our offices or at the hospital all day, then went to classes three nights a week, from 8.30 to 10.00 pm. The instructors assigned many articles to be read for each course every session, which forced us students to essentially spend most of the weekend reading the assigned works. We read a great deal of Freud, of course, but also many others, essentially reviewing a significant number of what was written, mostly by Freudians, though we also read some Melanie Klein, Winnicott, Bion, etc., from 1900 to 1970s. The readings and the interactions with the teachers, as well as the supervisions, contributed to the feeling of being in possession of a kind of knowledge that gave us the tool to understand human behavior, normal or pathological, not only in a unique way, but in the only correct way. Consequently, there was no need to learn from other disciplines. Yes, reading good works of literature and poetry, or philosophy were useful because you could understand them better if you applied a psychoanalytic interpretation to them. At the time of my training and for years afterwards, being a psychoanalyst conveyed a certain prestige and all of these contributed to keeping the heavy door to the institute closed. We did not really need to know what was happening in neuroscience, behavioral psychology, and, for a period or time, not even psychopharmacology because they were nowhere close to finding what we already knew and applied to our treatment technique which was unique.

Anonymity, which I mentioned above, had another consequence. It conveyed a code of behavior. We could not be too visible, we could not go hang out in places where we would be seen by our patients, we could not misbehave in public, we could not socialize too broadly because we may run the risk of running into a patient in a social situation. Therefore, the safest was to socialize amongst ourselves, thus we had dinner parties of mostly psychoanalysts, went to restaurants, to concerts as a group, and developed a sense of being one big family and, like all big families, there were shifting sides, in and out of favor, the good group and less good group, and so on. But as psychoanalysts we stuck together even if we had theoretical disagreements. To move up the ladder at NYPSI and reach the exulted status of Training Analyst (one who can treat psychoanalytic candidates) was the ultimate goal. I climbed the ladder pretty fast. I graduated after finishing the four-year curriculum, first one from my class to graduate, and became a member of the New York Psychoanalytic Institute and Society and of the American Psychoanalytic Association, and became a certified psychoanalyst by 1980 and, I think, was appointed a Training Analyst in the mid-eighties. Unbeknownst to most people outside the psychoanalytic groups, being appointed a Training Analyst was a big deal. In fact, the majority of the fights at the institute or even at the American Psychoanalytic Association were about this rite of passage. To be a psychoanalyst was one thing, but to be a Training Analyst a much higher achievement. As usual, such titles are often accompanied by a lot of infighting, being careful in not making too many enemies, and sometimes being friends with the right subgroups. And again, as often happens in all organizations, especially where prestige plays a role, some get appointed who are deserving, and some who are not but, most importantly, some do not get appointed who are deserving but have either unknowingly irritated some people or have been on the wrong side.

Going back to me, simultaneously to being named Training Analyst, I moved up along the administrative ladder, having been already the Treasurer, I became president of the Society, then Chair of the Faculty and finally Chairman of the Education committee, the highest position at NYPSI. I also became involved in the national and international associations and made many friends, nationally and internationally. Psychoanalysis was my life, next to my family life, though I can say now that the latter suffered from my active involvement. For years I went to the institute three to four nights a week after work, for teaching and sitting in or running committees.

The building on 82nd Street, with its squat solid appearance despite the deteriorating condition inside, became for me, and perhaps for us members of the institute, more than a place with classrooms, auditorium, library, and administrative offices. It was our intellectual, professional, aspirational, and social home; it was our castle, it was our fort. In it were our seniors, with their seniors, and the deceased seniors. The thoughts, the rules, the disagreements, the principles, the traditions, all lived within those walls and created a continuity from decade to decade. The study groups that had started years ago continued. The chairmen changed, group members changed or died, but the Kris study group continued; same with the scientific meetings, once a month on Tuesday year after year after year. Everything was connected along a long cord or rope, extending from the past to the present, and the cord got longer every year. Freud, of course, was there at all times. We had created his spiritual home and he lived with us. Statues, oil portraits, photographs, archives, he was in the building. There were other institutes, some with their own building, but it was only the New York Psychoanalytic Institute that mattered, it was our mecca, and we saw ourselves as the guardians of the true Freudian discoveries that we felt had changed the world, and in our role as psychoanalysts, we thought we were the best.

We all had two homes, one where we lived, and the institute. We worked hard to become and remain a member of the institute and we did not need to open our windows or doors to the rest of the world, especially the mental health world. We had the best answers, the best solutions, the best theory, and they all resided at 82nd street.

Freud was our leader. If we wanted to show that we were right, we said, "but Freud said that." To be in alignment with Freud, defend Freud, to show how superior he was, how he described the causes of all of human mental suffering, how he kept revising and fine-tuning his discoveries, was what made us feel we were "real psychoanalysts." Often, at our meetings or study groups, someone's name would pop out, a psychoanalyst from another institute, or from England or France, and someone would assert, "but he is not a real psychoanalyst." The same was said of psychoanalysts who devoted their time to running psychiatric hospitals. They were not real analysts because they did not see a sufficient number of patients in psychoanalysis. In sum, we analysts from the New York Psychoanalytic Institute embodied Freud. This does not mean that there were no theoretical and clinical disagreements, but they all had Freud's understanding and theories of the mind as their foundation.

This was the culture, this was the atmosphere in those days, but nevertheless, I sometimes wonder, these days, if my own background did not make me susceptible to maintaining this intense degree of allegiance.

I mentioned above my separation from first wife in 1974. I remained single until mid 1976, when I met my current wife. Soon after our meeting, we spent all our free time together and then married in 1981. We had planned to marry in 1979, but my father, who had moved to New York with my mother in 1977, died in August of '79, and it was not considered appropriate for me to marry until a year had passed. The next plan, to get married in 1980, became problematic because I found a swelling on my neck which was diagnosed tentatively as cancer of the salivary gland. The physician, who had already missed my father's cardiac infarct diagnosis, but who was an infectious disease specialist, diagnosed it. Of course, he did not give me a thorough anamnesis and did not even do blood work. Once he felt the lump, he made the diagnosis. The surgeon I saw was a very competent and distinguished surgeon. He assumed the previous physician had done all the necessary workup and come to the diagnosis therefore he immediately, with no further exam except the touching of the node, scheduled the surgery. I was lying in the hospital bed the day after the operation, which had not been eventful except for some difficulty waking up after the anesthesia, that the surgeon walked in and told my wife and I that there was no cancer but that I had Toxoplasmosis. A word about Toxoplasmosis is in order since not everyone is familiar with the condition. I had learned about it during medical school, and it is a relatively frequent infection in Europe, particularly in Belgium and France where raw meat is consumed. Steak tartare is in fact a very popular dish in Belgium. Toxoplasmosis is caused by a parasite that resides in raw meat, and is particularly dangerous during pregnancy, and if it ends up infecting vital organs such as the eye.

Because of the threatening nature of the diagnosis of cancer of the salivary gland, I asked my fiancé to postpone the marriage, and told her that I would not subject her to a marriage with someone with a serious illness. we postponed the marriage tentatively until early January 1981 but since the diagnosis ended up being benign, we did marry on that date. A year and a half later, October 1982 we had our daughter. Unfortunately, three weeks before her birth, my wife was diagnosed with Toxoplasmosis which can be very dangerous for the fetus. However, after three months of treatment of the newborn without a diagnosis, since it takes around three months before the diagnostic test could be considered valid, and after my consulting all the top experts around the world, in Europe and South America especially, where they are much more familiar with it, we discovered that my daughter was not exposed to it. She grew up without any health issues and, being the youngest, had my mother almost all to herself—which was very gratifying to my mother. I was now the father of two girls and a boy. My wife and my three children and my mother were all the family I had in New York. I had no ongoing connection to Iran or Armenia. I knew no one from those old countries. My world was New York and my small family. In some way, being separated from my roots from early on, this was always how my life had been.

Recently, I was reading my father's short and incomplete biography, which he wrote towards the end of his life after his stroke, and that my wife had had translated from Armenian. Though I can read and write in Armenian, not having done so on a regular basis has made it much harder for me to read, especially because the absence of punctuation makes it so that one has to read each word and the sentence correctly. Given my father's handwriting and the sequela of his stroke on his cognition, reading it in Armenian and understanding it fully was not possible for me. In the English translation, not so well done, I found out about my father's reflections on his roots as he was confronting mortality. I remember when I was a boy in Tehran, there was a small shop down the street from the Armenian church that lent Armenian books, and both my parents would borrow books from there. An old Armenian, Sako, with a large collection of all types of books written in Armenian, from history to novels to poetry, owned the store. It was the main source of books for the Armenians in Tehran. Apparently, at some point, my father or mother had come across a small book that spoke about my father's great-great-grandparents. The book reports on the writings of Melik Shego, the son of Melik Kishmir, who is the oldest member of the clan my father was told about. My father then describes in his biography the descendants of Melik Shego and their marriages, and where they lived, and what they did, the properties they owned, the education they had, the battles they participated in, the charitable work they did, their prominence (Melik in Armenian denotes a noble title). One of Melik Shego's sons, was a Melik Davit who was my father's grandfather; his son Nersess was my father's father. My father talks a bit about his grandfather whom he remembers, and about his father who died from pneumonia when my father was about eight years old. He recalls being taken to his dying father's bedside, being kissed by him on the forehead, and his father then turning to my father's uncle and saying "Make sure Khachik (short form of my father's name, Khachatour) gets an education, whatever the cost may be. I am dying now; this will be your duty." It is no wonder that education was my father's number one priority. Another priority was freedom, having to some extent lost his since he could not return to Armenia. He once told me for every language you speak, you are yet another person. I speak four, plus manage in another. I am writing all this, however, for another reason. As I have been thinking about and remembering my relationship with the New York Psychoanalytic Institute, I have been having these questions in my mind about the intensity of the involvement. Why was it my second home? The obvious answer, and probably the correct one, is that this is how things were then, and not just me, but all of us New York Psychoanalytic members felt the same way, and committed with the same intensity. The less obvious answer, and perhaps it is totally barking up the wrong tree, is that it may have something to do with my life history.

My father had been separated from his home and his past and forbidden to go back to it, we lived in Iran which, though extremely hospitable, was not our ancestral home. We were welcome guests, but guests, nevertheless. I went to England for education, and I was a foreigner, then Belgium, where the term foreigner was rarely used, but being catholic was important, then Canada and then the U.S. where I felt welcomed. This lack of visible, tangible roots—Could it have made me more susceptible to fully embracing the home on 82nd Street? I don't know. The fact is I never felt out of place or truly unwelcome except on a few occasions in England, but the fact also is that I really have no roots. When I went to Armenia for a week in 1984 and met the large Armenian family, I was very happy but did not feel I really belonged; I was a guest. The cord or rope that connected the psychoanalysts of the New York Institute that I mentioned above, going from Freud to the next generation and then the next, and eventually my generation, did not really exist in my personal life. I guess my father in his old age was trying to re-establish that continuity which he had experienced but which had been interrupted for most of his life thanks to Stalin and especially Beria. He always expressed disdain if not hatred for them, especially Beria.

In any case, Psychoanalysis and the New York Psychoanalytic Institute were central to my life, and gave me a sense of being a part of a group, and of an idea or belief of being the practitioner of a method that changed people's lives, and also a theory that explained how the human mind worked. I believe this was also true of others who, like me, had left their homes—immigrants mostly from Europe, escaping the holocaust.

REFERENCES

Freud, S. (1909). Notes upon a Case of Obsessional Neurosis. *Standard Edition*, Volume X:153–249.

——— (1917). Mourning and Melancholia. *Standard Edition*, Volume XIV:243–258.

——— (1918). From The History of an Infantile Neurosis. *Standard Edition*, Volume XVII:7–122

CHAPTER 5

A Christmas Day Eve in My Office

My office is grey, the walls and the ceiling and the bookcases are all painted grey. It is light, as light as a Manhattan townhouse (which is also my home) room can be. There are three windows, two floor-to-ceiling French windows facing the street and a smaller side window. I am on the South side of the street. The sun shines in at certain times of the day. The wall between the French windows has a framed drawing hanging on it. I sit in front of the West window, and under the drawing on the wall is the couch. A chair faces the couch about six feet away. The other walls, except the one above the fireplace on the East side, have built in bookcases. There is a small wall in front of where I sit that has no bookcase and a photograph of Robert Penn Warren by Annie Liebowitz hangs there. I have been sitting in the same corner of the room for 40 years. Nowadays I don't work more than a maximum of 8 hours a day, but in the past, I sometimes worked 12 to 14-hour days.

On December 25, 2017, at the end of the day, I felt like I had had too much stimulation. Christmas days are very joyous but packed, packed with noise, packed with presents, packed with work, just packed. My children and grandchildren come, my wife, having spent endless hours satisfying everybody's wishes, has piles of presents under the tree, and on Christmas morning two to three hours is spent opening gifts. Only my wife is allowed to buy me gifts; the three children can jointly only buy me a subscription to *Science* magazine. After everyone has opened their gifts, and almost all the time, they have most of their wishes satisfied, we have brunch, and soon after work to prepare a big dinner. So, by the time everyone goes to bed, a lot has happened, and being on overload is not surprising. On this particular Christmas day night, as I was walking upstairs to go to my bedroom floor, I felt an urge to go into my office, and I sat there for some time. It felt warm, comfortable, giving myself time to decompress slowly. Feeling things in my chest, my gut, my head that I could not put a name to. I looked at the photograph of Robert Penn Warren hanging on the wall in front of my chair, and he is sitting on his bed, bare chested, looking at the camera, and it just amplified the feeling or feelings with no name.

There have been, since the days of William James, a great many studies done on emotions; James's four main emotions have morphed into 6, and then 27, and then primary and secondary, and then pure and combined, and so on. Even in Wikipedia you can see the evolution of the increasing complexity and also a lack of complete clarity in trying to definitely understand an important part of who we are. Joseph Ledoux, who has done pioneering work on emotions, has recently proposed that it is the cognitive assessment of the emotion, that is to say the conscious perception of the emotion, that is important and explains why tackling fear, for example, by targeting the amygdala, does not always bear fruit. If conscious perception is important then, for reasons that I know nothing about, we have no language for something that we are feeling and are conscious of but don't know exactly what it is.

On that Christmas Eve, as I said, I was feeling a lot but did not know what. It was not melancholic though there was a bit of that, it wasn't joy though there was a bit of that too, it was something that just by sitting in my office, which was lit but the light is never very bright, after some ten or fifteen minutes, subsided, and I felt I wanted to go up to the bedroom.

It is after that night that I began to realize that I am in an emotional state at the end of my work day, and that this state has no name. Psychoanalysis is not unique as a field of medicine to create all sorts of emotions in the practitioner, but it is unique in that there are no distractions, I cannot say, yes, my patient is distressed because of the migraine but I can prescribe something to take care of it. In psychoanalysis I sit in the emotion with the patient, I consciously, but more often unconsciously, respond to my patient's feelings during the fifty minutes of the session, and then I sit with the feelings of the next patient. All day I am responding to emotions and then, at the end, I feel something that has no name. In fact, I don't know of the existence of this something until I have been away from work for a substantial period of time. At least this is what I have come to recognize now, as I am considering seriously the end of my career, just as I was responding to the end of the day on that Christmas day night.

My grey office, my books, the chairs, the art, and my relationship with my patients are all part of me, not just metaphorically but as if concretely. Early in my work, it was not so. I was distancing myself; I was thinking: What interpretation should I make? Is the one I made correct? Will the patient respond positively or will she or he reject it? Sometimes I would fantasize during the hour of other things, think of what I was teaching, or some administrative issue or problem, think about the weekend or an upcoming vacation, but now I don't. When I sit in my chair it is as if everything is in one piece, I am cognizant of other things, of course, but I don't think about them, and I have a feeling state that has no name. I look at Penn Warren and think maybe we are feeling the same way. When I bought the photograph some thirty years ago, he seemed old, not so much now. He has a look of irony and perhaps even a bit of distance, but I don't see curiosity. It makes me wonder if, after a while, curiosity loses its hold on us. Yet, curiosity is what sustains me in my daily work, and curiosity, or more precisely its role in psychoanalytic work, is what helped me be placed on the road to question some and gradually a great deal of Freudian theory. Fetishism is another catalyst earlier on in my career but more about that later.

On the face of it, curiosity, it would seem, would be an obvious psychoanalytic instrument (a term used in psychoanalysis to define the various tools a psychoanalyst has at his disposal such as listening, interpreting etc.). However, during my training and my early years as a psychoanalyst, curiosity or talking about it was unwelcome. The reasons for this were twofold: first and most importantly, curiosity was considered as closely associated to voyeurism, that is to say a desire to look for the purpose of the satisfaction of a sexual impulse, therefore psychoanalysts could not be curious because then they would be voyeuristic. Second, the mental posture the psychoanalyst was supposed to have was one of being like a sponge, allowing the patients thoughts to be soaked in, and then automatically an interpretation would form in his head, almost without conscious effort, and then this understanding would be communicated to the patient, either for therapeutic benefit or to facilitate the flow of further associations. In fact, some even claimed that asking questions was not conducive to the work since the idea was just to follow the flow of free associations. The problem, of course, was that the thought that came to the analyst's mind, which then led to the interpretation, was always based on the theory, such as primal scene fantasies, oedipal conflict, forbidden erotic or aggressive fantasies, and so on.

Though free associations sounded good on paper, in practice no one truly free associated, and in fact, if they did it would be difficult to decipher anything. This is why some had created another term called free communications, that is to say the patient was to tell the psychoanalyst her/his thoughts without or with as little censoring as possible.

The idea that curiosity is an important ally in understanding an analysand came to me, I am sure, over time. I don't believe it was an aha moment, but there is one situation that stays on my mind in this regard, and which certainly was an important catalyst in my thinking about psychoanalytic technique taking this particular direction.

The young woman was about thirty years old when she came to see me. She suffered from a sense of generalized malaise, she lived with her mother, worked as a secretary despite having been to top NYC private schools and a good college, did not have a boyfriend and just felt that she did not see anything to look forward to in her future. After a few meetings, I suggested we undertake five times a week psychoanalysis and, after consultation with her mother, she agreed.

I should warn at this point, that what I am describing, and in a very outline form, may not be all accurate in every detail, since I am only remembering this patient and the circumstances I will describe below. Memory, particularly autobiographic memory, is unreliable and subject to distortions (Alberini, 2013). However, I think the main part of the story is accurate. Over the years of this analysis, I obviously discovered many things about my patient, one of these was that her parents separated and divorced when she was about ten years old, and her father went back to Europe, and her mother prevented her from seeing him or communicating with him. She, of course, had many fantasies about her father, some of them stimulated by what she had heard her mother say about him. In the analysis therefore, he was presented and seen as this dashing, handsome playboy who drove Ferraris and lived a jet-setter's life. At some point in the more advanced stages of the analysis, and as a result of the work, she overcame her inhibitions and sent him a letter, thinking he would never respond. She received an immediate response inviting her to go visit him. She did, and upon her return described what she had seen and experienced, and the fact that her father had a heart condition, and how he was not able to be as active as he would have liked because of his old age. He was in his seventies at that point. Upon hearing this, I realized how my curiosity had failed me or rather I had had no curiosity, for had I had any about her father, I would have recognized that the fantasies she was having about him may have been possible years ago but not when we were working on her feelings about this playboy father of the present. I had not said to myself that by now he must be an old man. I was taken aback by my lack of genuine curiosity about this matter. That does not mean that analyzing her fantasies had not been helpful, they had been very helpful indeed, but at some point, for her and me to realize that we were talking about what was rather than what is—namely that now her father was an old man—would have been helpful. The more important point, however, is the absence of my curiosity.

This is how it coalesced in my mind then, a chance event and a recognition that I had been blind.

Of course, curiosity for the therapist, as I have come to view it, is to tolerate ignorance and to not fit a patient's communications into preconceived formulas. What I mean by this is that, in the time of my training and in the years that followed it, I listened to the patient and my curiosity was focused on looking for evidence that I could use to interpret to the patient, for example her or his oedipal conflict. In other words, my curiosity was a directed curiosity, a direction dictated by my theoretical viewpoint which, in my case, was what was called *classical Freudian*. To put it another way, I looked for things that were based on the theory I would find or formulated; the meaning of what the patient said was according to the theory; my curiosity was a prisoner of the theory. Not free, not truly curious, not exploring with no preconceived ideas, but following a direction given to me and to we psychoanalysts of the New York Psychoanalytic Institute, by Freud and his followers. Now, when I was shocked into becoming aware of how much I did not see because I thought I had the roadmap, overtime I decided to free myself from the theory. As I will make it clear later, I also set on a path that, over the years, would make me question the Freudian edifice. Enough said about curiosity, but maybe another word about fitting observations into preconceived theory. The same patient would go through periods when everything would seem like too much to bear, she would miss sessions, have nothing to say during the hour and feel essentially blah. I would report this to my supervisor, who would say these states represented her resistance to recognizing the intensity of her loving and sexual feelings in the relationship with me. In psychoanalytic jargon, she was defending against her sexual and loving feelings, originally towards her father but now towards me, which had been activated in analysis, that is to say she had transferred those repressed feelings to me and was now fighting them. Therefore, when she would say she had a hard time just climbing the one floor of steps to my office, that it was a defense against these same erotic impulses. I interpreted this to her numerous times, not much changed. The reality is the patient suffered with bouts of depression, and what she was describing were classical symptoms of depression, yet I was fitting her into the theory.

Parenthetically here, as I will describe in a bit more detail later, psychoanalysis does not have a theory of emotion, and this is because for Freud, "affect" which is the translated term, was very closely connected to drive, and since in his theory there were only two drives, sexual and destructive, all emotion was viewed as expressions of these two. Anger, rage, and fear related to the aggressive drive, and sexual longing, love, and desire connected to the sexual drive.

In remembering these incidents, and there are many others, of course, it is good to keep in mind that these realizations about the problems in theory and technique had a long gestation period in me, and it is only with hindsight that they seem so obvious and so regretful. My commitment to Freudian theory for the first two and half decades of my career in psychoanalysis was unwavering.

Going back to the subject of emotions, I see many questions. How intense does an emotion have to be before we are aware of it or we can give it a name? How many emotions are there for which we have no name? What emotions sometimes appear as other emotions, for example a feeling of depression representing anxiety? How do various emotions interact? And also, as Ledoux has recently tried to tackle, how to understand consciousness as it relates to emotions? Is awareness of ones thoughts the same as awareness of feelings? Or is awareness of the world, the same as awareness of our feelings? Antonio Damasio has described how emotions originate in the body, they are primarily reactions of the organs of the body, heart, muscles, abdomen that are then perceived by the brain and we become aware of them as feelings. Feelings of fear, love, sorrow, joy. Related to this idea, I am beginning to think to what degree cognition is driven by emotion rather than the other way around and more importantly that action is driven by emotion rather than cognition in a larger number of instances than we usually assume. This is interesting especially because there are emotions that we have not clearly defined, and some we have not even given a name to, and yet they may be determining our thoughts, actions, behaviors and moods. Another issue of interest is the role emotions play in memory consolidation. This last point could mean that some memories are stored and then consolidated, not based on similarity of content but on emotional factors, and this could explain certain juxtapositions we see in dreams where on the face of it they seem illogical or totally unrelated. This may well be where Freud's ideas about how to work with dreams and how to interpret them could be used for memory research purposes. For Freud and psychoanalysts, the linking of dream elements based on the underlying emotion rather than the ideational content is part of the work of dream interpretation. I have also been asking myself if emotions are the true instigators of dreams, and I increasingly think they are.

My assertion above that many of our actions may be primarily emotion driven rather than cognition driven seems at one level obvious. For example, if we see a car speeding our way we step back even before we actually think, however, there are many instances where it may seem that our or others actions are cognitively based, yet on examination may reveal the more powerful emotional underpinning. I am also saying emotion more often leads to thought, and possibly action, than thought leads to emotion. I am aware, of course, that I can think of a certain event or possibility and then feel one way or the other, but I am beginning to think the balance is most often in the other direction.

REFERENCES

Alberini, C.M., Ed. (2013). *Memory Reconsolidation*. Academic Press.

Nersessian, E. (1995). Some Reflection on Curiosity and Analytic Technique. *Psychoanalytic Quarterly* LXIV, Vol.1: pp. 113–135.

CHAPTER 6

The Start of Questioning Freud

September 11, 2001 is a date the world remembers and, of course, we in New York have that day and the days following it when the aura of death hung over Manhattan, etched in our minds indelibly. I remember in detail how I first heard about it during a session when it was considered an accident involving a small plane, then afterwards going to the television and seeing the film of the first large jet plane and then the second plane. I also remember, in most of my senses, going to the armory where families were bringing certain belongings of sons, daughters, fathers, mothers and other kin, who were in the twin towers, to have their DNA checked, and where, as a psychiatrist, I talked to those who were open to speak to me. I remember leaving my office, located between Park and Madison Avenues, that morning, and seeing Park Avenue deserted. No taxis, no cars; finally I was able to get a lift from another doctor who was also going downtown.

I don't have the skills to describe accurately what that period of time was like in New York, and I am sure it has been described in much more emotionally accurate ways by others; I only mention it because that date has become a kind of a time-post for people of this generation who witnessed it, and so I remember, like most New Yorkers, and many people around the world: the before and the after. My own emotions on the day it happened, and on the next day when I went to the armory are lost. Not all, I remember the fear I felt until we found out my son had not gone for his training to the

World Trade Center that day, and he was ok. Finding later that a friend's daughter had been there and had died, and the sense of sorrow, but the bulk of the emotions I felt I cannot name. It was a state of being; it was me going down with a car to the Armory, and it was not me. My body below my skin seemed suddenly to be more present, and while some feelings like fear, anxiety, dread, sorrow were present and identifiable by me, others were just bathing me but from inside. I don't even know if what I just wrote is understandable but, whereas a bathwater covers one from the outside of the skin, these feelings took hold of my whole person from inside.

Then my behavior over the next months changed. I suddenly seemed to be much more focused on food, and specifically repeatedly cooking for my children and wife. Even guests noticed the intensity of my engagement in providing food and cooking. Nameless emotions controlled my behavior . Slowly and increasingly, I began to feel acutely the need for independence, self-sufficiency, and competence in the way I ran my life. I also began to have a different sense about my work with patients, I began to weigh carefully everything I thought and said, and started reassessing my knowledge. Whether these changes in my person had anything to do with my increased skepticism about what I read in psychoanalysis and what I heard, I cannot be sure. The speculations presented as certainty, in clinical conferences, began to bother me more, and when I read, I saw the contradictions, and the proofless claims more vividly. My starting work with the Philoctetes Center, which I will describe later, also had a very major role in my gradual conversion from a very classical Freudian to a skeptic, and to where I am now writing these pages.

My gradual movement away from much of Freud's theories, I know did not begin immediately; rather, it gradually evolved but it did mostly happen in the 21st century.

I am making this assertion despite the fact that I can see, looking back, that seeds of doubt and disagreement can be seen in the paper I wrote on

Fetishism which was published in 1998. I had been treating a woman who had many phobias, and her relationship with her husband appeared to be based on her need to cling to someone who would protect her from her fears. She had a hard time trusting anyone, had had a number of therapists before me, and even when seeing me, only after a couple of years did she reveal that she was going to stop seeing a second therapist she had been seeing during the whole time she was in therapy with me but had never told me about. There were many interesting features in this case, which are described in the paper, and which I will not go into here. For those interested, a reference to the paper is given in the back of this book, also, the conclusions I came to in the paper may or not really be valid. The paper was published in 1998, and I was very much a believer in Freud's theories at the time. My conclusions, which I will mention, only to show that I was beginning, without my knowledge, to diverge from some of Freud's ideas, were that one: fetishism was not only present in males, and that two: it belonged to the many ways different people handle anxiety. This is how I put it in the paper: "Fetishism is a particular manifestation of a more general tendency in which some 'thing,' some concrete, tangible object, is used as an aid in controlling anxiety." I then stepped back, as it were, and made a broader assertion: "My data …" (you realize it is so limited, it seems to me today almost embarrassing to use the term *data,* but for what is worth, I continued) "… also suggest theoretical flaws in stringent adherence to the idea that fetishism is almost solely a male phenomenon deriving primarily from intense castration anxiety. Such a view overlooks the importance of all the so-called hierarchical anxieties in the use of a fetish, anxieties that are common to both men and women in their early development, and that continue throughout life. Although there are undeniable biological, physiological, hormonal, anatomical, and experiential differences between the sexes, there are equally undeniable similarities in their psychological development."

Where was I differing from Freud? This is what he said in 1928: "To put it more plainly: The fetish is a substitute for the woman's (mother's) penis that the little boy once believed in and—for reasons familiar to us—does not want to give up." The reasons familiar to us refers to castration anxiety. Freud then postulated that a mechanism called disavowal is at work which allows the person to both know and not know, i.e., that the woman has a penis and does not have a penis. In other words to summarize Freud's hypothesis:

"The fetish is closely related to castration anxiety. At the cost of a fracture in reality testing (by a mechanism called disavowal) the fetish provides a solution to the fact that the woman does not have a penis and is invariably accompanied by the fantasy of a phallic woman (i.e., a woman who has a penis)."

At the time of writing this paper, I did not think I was in any way questioning Freud's assertions, in other words, I still believed in the existence of the phallic woman fantasies in men, as well as the idea that the sight of the vagina caused castration anxiety in them. What I thought I was doing was to broaden the concept of fetishism and to assert that it is a more generalized phenomena having to do with how both men and women use others or objects to control their anxieties of whatever source the anxiety may be. In fact, around the same period, I was analyzing a man with a foot fetish who I thought had a childhood memory of the type we call screen memory (i.e., it is screening other memories or fantasies) that pointed to his fear of losing his penis and, therefore, I understood his fetishism in classic Freudian ways.

What I did become aware of, however, at that time, and this may have worked on my mind subliminally for years, is that Freud avoided giving clinical examples except for one tiny vignette. This struck me; did he have many more cases he was not describing due to confidentiality issues (which he asserted), or was he making large claims out of a limited set of data? This brought to mind that when I was working on the *Textbook of Psychoanalysis* with my friend and colleague Richard Kopff, we asked the author of one of the papers if the explanation he gave of a female patient's plane phobia being connected to the penis, and the fact that the steering of the plane is called the joy stick, was because the patient had made the connection. He said no, he had made the connection and interpreted it. To psychoanalysts in those days, if what they heard could fit a schema originally described by Freud, then that interpretation was correct. The textbook, published by the American Psychiatric Press was published relatively early in my career and, luckily, was a success enough so that some years later it was republished and edited by another psychoanalyst.

While writing this chapter, I went to an event one evening in Brooklyn. It was supposed to be on the importance of silence. Here is how it was described:

"Long before John Cage's infamous 4'33" made an entire piece out of silence, composers have used rests and pauses to bring their music to life. Now, these brilliant creators and thinkers are delving into the secrets of silence, melding dynamic art and cutting-edge science into a captivating whole."

I was told about the event in which he was participating, by a friend, Joseph Ledoux. Joe is a neuroscientist of incredible scientific integrity, to whom validating data over and over is extremely important. In addition to Ledoux, three other people presented; one was a musician and psychotherapist, and another a psychoanalyst. The psychoanalyst presented a paper on the importance of silence in psychoanalysis, and at one point quoted, with great admiration, the paper of a colleague wherein the colleague described a patient who remained silent during a whole hour, and so the psychoanalyst also remained silent. Not an unusual recommendation by supervisors when I was a student, and later, to do as this analyst did. The analyst then spoke about how the next sessions revealed that this was a life-changing event for this patient. This was reported by the presenter with great admiration and strong conviction, perhaps even a touch of self-congratulation for believing in this assertion and the great value of silence. There was no touch of doubt, questioning or irony; this is what the analyst had reported and thus it was the truth. No modesty about the fact that life changing is a huge assertion, and a conviction in the presenter that this treatment modality i.e., psychoanalysis could, through a 50 minute silence, change a life. Psychoanalysis does change life's course when it is successful, but it takes years, not a session, and what actually causes the change is debatable, and I will present my take on it later. But the point here is that our allegiance to psychoanalysis and our belief in our theories, in my case, Freudian, was such that serious validation of data was not something we thought about. The example I just gave is an exaggerated version, though not by much, of the innumerable case reports I heard whether when I was very active in the IPA, or APsA, or NYPSI, or at private study groups. All sorts of claims were made on scant evidence and we spent hours and hours discussing and debating them, taking sides, asserting our views, or just saying nothing. It is no question that for years, for me, these meetings, by and large, with some exceptions, were highly interesting. The clinical cases presented from various countries, by analysts from different countries and different theoretical allegiances, were educative, and I learnt a great deal within not just the psychoanalytic field but about different cultures in general. Listening to Argentinian, Peruvian, Brazilian, French, Italian, Spanish, German, Japanese, etc. analysts also gave the listener a glimpse of these different cultures which was enriching. So was meeting all the analysts from these various countries, socializing with them and learning. This issue of conviction reminds me of a time when the chairman of the faculty at NYPSI asked me to present my ideas, that is to say, my critique of Freud at a faculty meeting. He had also asked two other colleagues to present clinical cases to show the validity of Freud's assertions. After I presented, an old supervisee of mine presented the case of a child to show his disagreement with my propositions. He essentially recited all the known formulas which he had applied to the understanding of the patient: oedipal issues, childhood masturbation, fear of castration, and so on. He was so convinced in his formulations without any iota of doubt that I decided to keep silent, realizing that he was not taking distance from the theory and questioning it, but rather blindly espousing it, like we had all done for years, and like I had helped him do during supervision.

Going back, after this long digression, to my tentative and unverified hypothesis in this paper regarding Fetishism, it began to make me think about ways in which anxiety manifested itself, and not just in the usual psychoanalytic sense. One example is how, based on the case of one patient who felt down, despondent, pessimistic and without energy whenever he had to do something that made him anxious, even though what he was aware of was not anxiety but the feelings I mentioned, I hypothesized that anxiety can be behind other emotions, in particular depression. In other words anxiety does not necessarily only lead to symptoms such as compulsions but can lead to other emotions. Whether this is correct or not will be for emotion researchers to confirm or reject, but I mention it to say that, partly unknowingly, I began to focus a great deal on anxiety in my thinking about my work, and I tried to understand the neuroscience of it and Ledoux's work on fear was useful in this regard.

I should, in defense of this point, add that there is current research in psychiatry seeing anxiety as behind some depressions.

What I implied in the beginning of this chapter, I believe is at least partially accurate, namely, the trauma of September Eleventh, had a particular impact on me, and one aspect of that impact was a more independent stance accompanied by a consistent questioning of everything I read in Freud's and other analysts' work. It was as if I was looking more acutely for facts and valid data than before.

CHAPTER 7

Neuroscience, Philoctetes, and Helix

On December 11, 2008 I went to check my emails between two sessions with patients. I saw an email from my son Greg, informing me that Bernie Madoff was arrested. My reaction was to feel numb for a few minutes, and then I had to continue my work, but the consequences of his arrest, which took some time for me to realize, were extremely important to me and I will describe it shortly, but first a little background.

In the early eighties I read *The Self and Its Brain* by Karl Popper and John Eccles. I had obviously studied some of Eccles work on the neurophysiology of synaptic transmission at medical school but didn't know of Karl Popper, the famous philosopher. After reading the book, I realized that in my work as psychoanalyst, I had totally forgotten the brain, and so I became totally engrossed by the book and found it an eye opener. I was also struck by Popper's ideas about falsifiability namely that a theory is only scientific if it is falsifiable. Later I became aware of his criticism of Psychoanalysis on this ground. I had, of course, totally espoused Freud's psychoanalysis and assumed that if we were in line with Freud's thinking, and we as psychoanalysts saw more or else the same issues and had more or less the same explanations, then psychoanalysis was science—a point of view that I no longer espouse, and which I am attempting to present in this book. Around this period, one of the senior members of the institute, Arnold Pfeffer, was planning to form a group with the help of an eminent neuroscientist and co-author with Eric

Kandel of a textbook on neuroscience, James Schwartz, in order to facilitate a dialogue between the two disciplines. He invited me to join, and we began a series of meetings on a monthly basis conversing with guests invited by Jimmy. A couple of years into this program, Arnold organized a second group with another neuroscientist, Jason Brown, and a neuropsychologist who was training in London to become a psychoanalyst, Mark Solms. Mark and I ended up essentially running the program and created the *Journal of Neuropsychoanalysis* with the clear ambition of approaching the two areas of study of the brain. The journal was published by IUP which, at the time, was one of the main publishers of psychoanalytic journals and books. It was owned by Martin Azarian and ran by him and his wife Margaret Emery. The reason for mentioning the neuroscience-psychoanalysis group, is not to go into the history of this particular endeavor but to describe what I saw in the meetings. What I saw—and it surprised me enormously at the time—were two things: One, neuroscientists did not really speak with each other and were narrowly focused on their particular research and area of expertise; And two, that they were not too open to take any of our ideas in and maybe draw additional conclusions from their observations, because, grants are narrowly defined especially as to the end point and, therefore, they did not pay much attention to what was outside the narrow scope of a particular grant. This point was made explicitly by Michael Gazzaniga when, during one of our meetings, I asked him about why a line of inquiry in a split brain patient was not pursued further in a particular direction. It was a direction I felt would reveal more about the person's psychic conflict which, of course, was not part of the scope of the grant but was of interest to a psychoanalyst.

During the period I have just described, I was given the task of revisiting the feasibility of creating a New York Psychoanalytic Foundation for fund-raising purposes by the then chairman of the Education Committee. The idea of a foundation had come up on a number of occasions in past years but was always voted down. The reason given, in every rejection of the idea, was the danger of contamination of the transference and the negative effects a foundation, made up of lay people, would have on the principle of abstinence which is related to anonymity and neutrality.

I think it makes sense to offer a bit of clarification on these principles of psychoanalytic technique. Freud's main point was that the patient's needs and longings, by which he usually meant sexual and loving needs, should remain frustrated in the patient in order to encourage the patient to try to understand their origins and, therefore, not be gratified by the psychoanalyst. In other words, if a patient's sexual longing in the relationship with the analyst, which was considered a transference, meaning it was displaced from longings towards one of the parents, was responded to by the analyst, then there would be no possibility of deepening the understanding of the longing and appreciating its origins. This, of course, independent of all the important additional ethical considerations. This rule, namely abstinence, was, over time, to become much broader, and it included any kind of interaction with the patient outside of the purely clinical setting. So much so in fact, that some analysts considered the offering of congratulations or condolences to be transgressions. Somewhat related to this was the concept of neutrality, which meant that the analyst should not inject his views and positions in the sessions and, therefore, never take sides in order to maintain a neutral and non-biased position, allowing him to understand the patient. The analyst's views, opinions, or preferences would, it was believed, contaminate the field of exploration which was the person's mind. They could also be perceived as suggestions about how and what the analyst thought the patient should think or behave. The analyst's anonymity meaning his/her not revealing anything about themselves, their likings, dislikes, views, tastes, nonpsychoanalytic knowledge, etc. were considered essential, and connected to the rule of neutrality which was that the analyst should not take any position but should remain completely neutral. The notion of neutrality was later defined using the structural theory which stipulated that the mind was composed of three agencies: Ego, Id, and Superego, that is to say wishes, executive functions, and an agent that determined what was right or wrong, principally on a moral basis. In this model, neutrality was defined as taking an equidistant position from the three components of the mind.

Though in psychoanalysis, we often spoke of the importance of anonymity and neutrality, Freud did not actually use these specific terms, rather he described the ideas in these principles under the concept of "abstinence."

At the New York Psychoanalytic, anonymity was taken very seriously, so seriously in fact, that when I went to a restaurant with some friends, and in came a group of senior analysts from the institute, I was surprised because I thought: What if some of their patients were also eating at the restaurant and would see them? The reality of course, as I came to find out over many years, and as I became a senior member myself, was that there was a huge gap between what was taught and what was practiced. I often wondered if what was taught, that is to say the extreme prohibitive nature of it, was not a reaction to the indiscretions that had occurred frequently in the past. The chief culprit of course was Freud himself who socialized with some patients, took acquaintances into analysis and analyzed Anna Freud. However, others had also committed many indiscretions including having affairs with patients, accepting gifts and other favors, and so on.

Another important rule in medicine, and therefore in psychoanalysis, was confidentiality, so that revealing that someone was a patient was forbidden. This was adhered to such a degree that our analysts at the institute would not acknowledge us when we ran into them at the institute and, for us students, it was always very uncomfortable to find ourselves in the elevator with our analyst. This, of course, gave us psychoanalysts, and especially us members of the New York Psychoanalytic, a sense of righteousness and superiority. All this to say that any discussion about a foundation was a quasi-forbidden territory. I did accept the challenge, however, formed a committee with some very senior people on it, and we came up with a solution. Ex-patients could contribute financially to the foundation as long as they were not solicited by their psychoanalyst. This was not some ingenious plan and fifteen years earlier it would have been voted down, but the climate was changing and there was the beginning of anxiety about how we were going to sustain the Institute. Once the foundation was formed I was asked to become its president and, based on suggestions I received, I formed a committee of nonanalysts plus a couple of analysts. One of the members of this committee was a man named Francis Levy.

This long diversion brings me to the creation of the Philoctetes Center for the Study of Imagination, which was instrumental in my ability to be able to take some distance from psychoanalytic theory and to look at it with more informed eyes. Mr. L, a writer, wanted to create a center to study creativity, since I know nothing about the subject I proposed we hold a number of meetings with people from different fields, based on my experience with the neuroscience group, and seeing value in speaking to people who were from another discipline than mine, to see what they advise. We held three such meetings at my home. We had at each meeting an interdisciplinary group from scientists like Karl Pribram and Anthony Damasio, to actors and actresses, artists including Laurie Anderson, priests, rabbis, English scholars, professor Paul Fry, child creativity experts Paul Harris, mathematicians like Barry Mazur and philosophers. The result was the recognition that imagination was more conducive to study than creativity, which was often associated to genius. Even more interestingly, we discovered how enlightening, useful, and enjoyable these interdisciplinary meetings had been, and we decided that it should be one of the activities of the center to organize such exchanges.

Mr. Levy then funded our creation of the center. We rented the third floor of the institute, renovated it to fit our purpose of organizing roundtables, and inaugurated the "Philoctetes Center." Our roundtables were, most of the time, fascinating to me. I left every one of them having learnt something new and, without being aware of it, they were changing my outlook; it was as if they opened my eyes to the larger world which up until then had been the world of psychoanalysis. The degree to which they changed my outlook was huge. It was as if I had been looking through a tunnel and now suddenly I could see the world that existed outside that tunnel. There were many highlights to my experience with Philoctetes but I always remember with pleasure organizing a roundtable on the "Origin of Life" based on a book by a professor of mine from medical school who I had only seen on the podium and had admired his eloquence, energy, and knowledge, and who was one of the few Nobel-prize winners in Belgium, Professor Christian De Duve. He was also a professor at Rockefeller University, so when I invited him and told him he had been my professor in Louvain, he happily accepted to participate. Rightly or wrongly, I felt a certain sense of achievement in this.

When we had had the meetings in my house, I would serve a light buffet dinner with wine, and then we would begin the discussion, at Philoctetes we began doing it the same way. A light buffet in the green room followed by the meeting. After three or four of these, Mr. Levy did not think they were needed, and so we stopped the pre-meeting food and wine. Instead, I began to have a dinner party for the participants and other dinner guests after the meetings at my home, and I found them highly enjoyable because often the discussion begun at the roundtable continued in a more relaxed manner, with no audience and some wine, and not infrequently it dug deeper into the question as less public politesse was du jour. It felt like an honor to me that De Duve accepted to come for dinner; somehow it seemed to imply a new phase in my professional life.

In 2008, we had been active for some four or five years, and doing very well. We had extended our programs to include art shows and roundtables around art since Mr. Levy's wife Hallie Cohen was an artist and a professor of Art, and to include music which Jane Ira Bloom helped us with, and we had begun funding a number of research projects in neuroscience including one on memory led by Professor Cristina Alberini. Additionally, we were supporting New York Psychoanalytic by creating fellowships for their students who used the grant to pay for their tuition. I think it was, all in all, a very worthy project that we planned to continue developing with new projects and ideas. We even had a Philoctetes center in Paris, run by a French neurologist/psychoanalyst. With our roundtables, we were able to get very prominent people in their respective fields, including Nobel prize winners. To the present day, many of the center's programs are on YouTube.

An interesting observation about the center was that most of the participants at the round tables assumed that the majority of the audience were psychoanalysts because of the venue being at the Institute, but in fact we had very few psychoanalysts. It seemed that psychoanalysts had lost their curiosity and were content with what they knew, but also, the number of NYPSI members who went to the NYPSI monthly lectures had, by then, also been declining, and sometimes there were more audience members from other places than the Institute. In a way, one could say that this is understandable, because there was really no longer anything new to be said about psychoanalytic theory or practice. The latest idea being what was called self-disclosure, which meant the analyst no longer needed to maintain complete anonymity, or even neutrality (being equidistant from Id, Ego, Superego.) In the meantime, I had written a paper with a student of mine, Mathew Sylvan, in which we had asserted that when your mental posture in the analysis is one of wanting to know how the patient thinks and feels, reacts and behaves, and why—when you are totally curious about your patient—then you are inevitably neutral.

But what does Madoff have to do with all this? I had not heard about Madoff until Levy spoke about him and encouraged me to invest some money with him, which I did. In fact, I wondered why he did not meet with me in his office when I called him to ask him about investing, and instead invited me to his home in the evening. I met him, for the first time, in his apartment. He asked about my situation and, naively, I was ready to give him all my money to invest, but he declined and said he would only take a portion. In that he was honest and decent. Sometime later we had a roundtable on the "Future of the Stock Market" during which he asserted that there was no way one could get away with any mischief in the stock market because the SEC was hyper-vigilant and watchful. The evening of the roundtable, as we had the usual dinner in our home, Madoff and his wife came. He sat next to my wife who told me later he was quite uninteresting. When they were leaving, he saw my office, which is on the second floor of my home, and he went over and lied on the couch; his wife looked at me and said, "he really needs it." The important issue, however, is that the money that was funding Philoctetes, came from a foundation of Levy's parents, and all that money was with Madoff.

Philoctetes struggled for the next two years, but then Levy, who had a majority of his friends on the board, was able to convince the board to shut it down in June 2012 (or 2011).

Soon after the closing of Philoctetes, The president of the institute approached me and encouraged me to restart the project, and offered the space on the third floor. Unfortunately, a few weeks later he was offered a deal he could not refuse, given the financial needs of the institute, and he rented the space to a construction company that was involved in the work on the Second Avenue Subway. A friend of mine, Anthony Lowbeer, whose mother and step father were both analysts (I will write a bit more about Nicholas Young, his step-father later) came to the rescue and offered to renovate the institute auditorium so it would accommodate both lectures as well as roundtables, and as soon as that work was done, and the auditorium was named after his parents, we began the Helix Center, and Dr. Robert Penzer accepted to be Associate Director. The Helix Center continues to this day and, more recently, Dr. Gerald Hurowitz took the Associate Director's position when Dr. Penzer resigned.

It is hard to emphasize what an incredible experience it was for me to be involved with the Philoctetes and Helix Centers. It is probably not an exaggeration to assert that they changed my life. To sit with experts from all fields and listen to them talk about subjects that matter was a gradual eye opener for me. The lively discussions at the Center, and then during dinner at my home, were opening my eyes to seeing more, and more, and more.

At the Helix Center, not having access to the kind of funds we had at Philoctetes, we could not afford the same intensity of programming, but, nevertheless, the fascinating roundtables continue. Of note is that whereas, at Philoctetes, we were able to pay a nice honorarium to our participants, at Helix, we cannot, but this has not changed at all the willingness of people to participate, even coming from different states and countries.

A long way to describe my personal evolution and the impact of two events, September 11th, possibly, and the multi-disciplinary meetings, certainly. An evolution that was slow in coming, in fact even in 2009 I made the following assertion in a presentation that was later published on "Minding the Gap." Gap being the distance between classical Freudians and Interpersonal, Sullivanian, psychoanalysts: I think we would be making a mistake to consider that the theory of instinctual drives is no longer valid,". I then went on to quote a prominent neurobiologist Donald Pfaff who in his 1999 book: *Drive, Neurobiological and Molecular Mechanisms of Sexual Motivation* stated that:

"the estrogenic and progestin actions on the hypothalamic neurons set up a general drive state. This notion, in turn, opens the possibility that we have discovered neurobiological and molecular biological foundations for the biological aspects of Freud's concept of instinct or drive" (i.e., libido).

I then went on to say that I believed that:

"Current and future understanding of drives, as elucidated and enhanced by biological research, are and will be more nuanced than the simple notion of force Freud advanced, but I think they will remain relevant and essential to any understanding of motivation and behavior."

When I went to look for this presentation I was surprised that it was only ten years ago that I was standing in defense of Freud's drive theory, and essentially assuming neurobiology will support the basics of Freud's ideas while explaining them with the tools and findings of biology.

This is not what I have thought for some time now; I realize it is not 10 years, and I hesitate to guess how long, but at least 5 or 6 years. How and why this reassessment of Freud happened may have other determinants, unknown to myself, but conversations over time with a large number of scholars of various fields no doubt contributed significantly to it.

CHAPTER 8

Where Actual Discussions of Psychoanalysis Begin

I have, so far, perhaps too circuitously, attempted to set down the groundwork for dealing with the subject of this work, which is why I think it is time to move to Freud and what I find highly problematic in his theories. In brief, looking back, I find the seeds of my disagreements were planted with the paper on Fetishism, then reinforced by my stressing the role of curiosity in technique, followed by my involvement in the neuroscience group, and most importantly with the multidisciplinary exchanges at the Philoctetes and Helix Centers, and finally by connecting aggression to anxiety. This latter idea seems probably self-evident to most people, but it was not to me, or to my colleagues, and many circuitous routes were taken by Freud and other psychoanalysts to explain sadism, for instance.

However, before I write about my questioning of psychoanalytic theory, I would like to quote myself from a paper I presented to the Faculty of the New York Psychoanalytic Institute around 1990. I think it will show clearly where I was then, and where I am now, as I tackle the so-called main tenets of psychoanalytic theory. The quote is from a book (where the article mentioned above is published) I edited it along with Manuel Furer and Carmela Perri, under the title: *Controversies in Contemporary Psychoanalysis:*

"I have found Roger Penrose's way of putting theories in an ordered perspective a useful guide in thinking about psychoanalysis and feel that psychoanalysis, like physics, has some superb theories which have extraordinary power in enabling us to understand the mind, some useful theories, and some that need to be considered tentative at this time. Among the superb I would include the dynamic unconscious, infantile sexuality and the Oedipus complex, the dual instinct theory, the pleasure unpleasure principle, the ubiquitous nature of transference, and the meaning of dreams."

I then listed the other categories and after doing that I wrote:

"As scientists, we know that the theories I have included among the superb are just that, and that they have enormous range and accuracy to explain the data we obtain every day in our consulting room. We do not need more 'empirical' research to prove that transference exists, that dreams have meaning, that infantile sexuality is fact."

This was where I stood then but which I no longer espouse. There have been significant discussions and debates about the scientific standing of psychoanalysis over the years, and they continue to this day. Some, like myself at the time of the above quote, stressed that psychoanalysis is indeed a science, whereas others disagreed and placed it more within the humanities and felt psychoanalytic theory should not be concertized like science.

I will not dwell further on the subject except to insist that today, for me, psychoanalytic theory is *absolutely not scientific.*

In this chapter, I will start by tackling the notion of the "dynamic unconscious" and its *raison d'etre,* "repression." I will then, in subsequent chapters, deal with the two-instincts theory, sex and aggression, the psychosexual stages of development (infantile sexuality), the pleasure/ unpleasure principle, and finally "the interpretation of dreams."

The notion of the unconscious, as understood by neuroscientists, is different from Freud's dynamic unconscious. There are many things that we are unconscious of such as implicit knowledge, or forgotten memories that, in the right circumstance, we may recall; we are also unaware of a great deal of what is in our minds until we focus our attention on it or are made to focus our attention on it. Furthermore, all of our experiences, and their mark on our minds, are not accessible to us, but more about this last point later. The Freudian unconscious, on the other hand, is different because it pertains to feelings, memories, and desires that are forcefully and actively kept out of awareness; that is to say are repressed because they are deemed to be forbidden. This process of keeping out of consciousness is an active mechanism which in classical psychoanalytic theory requires force. Freud, as can be expected, given the centrality of repression in psychoanalytic theory, discusses or mentions it all throughout his work, sometimes with small shifts in emphasis. Here is how he wrote about it in 1914:

"The theory of repression is the corner-stone on which the whole structure of psychoanalysis rests. It is the most essential part of it; and yet it is nothing but a theoretical formulation of a phenomenon which may be observed as often as one pleases if one undertakes an analysis of a neurotic without resorting to hypnosis. In such cases one comes across a resistance which opposes the work of analysis and in order to frustrate it pleads a failure of memory" (*S.E.* pp.16–14).

The discovery of repression occurred relatively early in Freud's work. A small detour into those early years may be useful in putting the beginnings of psychoanalysis into context.

In the Fall of 1885, Freud, a young man impatiently in love, went to Paris on a grant. He had met Martha around three years before, fallen in love and, hoping to make a decent enough living in order to marry her. He wrote to her almost constantly and kept her informed of his experience of Paris. He had graduated from medical school in 1881, having taken his time, and had been encouraged by Ernst Brucke, one of the most prominent physiologists of that time, and in whose lab Freud had worked on a number of research projects in physiology, to leave and obtain a post in a hospital in order to be able to make an income and move on with his life and eventually get married. Brucke, along with the other leading physiologists of the time, Hermann von Helmholtz, Emil du Bois-Reymond, and Carl Ludwig, formed a group of like-minded thinkers who believed only chemical-physical forces are active in an organism.

Freud followed Brucke's advice and obtained a position in the hospital and, for some months, worked in the neuro-anatomy lab of Theodore Meynert, a very prominent psychiatrist and neuropathologist who believed that disturbances in brain functioning could be responsible for psychiatric conditions. As Freud writes in the "Autobiographical Study" for "pecuniary reasons," after some time in Meynert's lab, he decided to move away from work on neuro-anatomy, and go towards exploring nervous diseases. Finding himself disappointed with the absence of a real field of neurology in Vienna, he began to hope he could spend some time with Charcot at the Salpetriere hospital in Paris.

Jean-Martin Charcot, considered the father of neurology by some, was a towering figure in Paris, and Freud was dazzled and influenced by him. His brief contact with the "great man" had such an impact that he named his first son Jean-Martin, later only referred to as Martin Freud. Charcot used hypnosis to induce symptoms and to remove symptoms such as arm paralysis, torticollis, and limb contractures in patients diagnosed as having hysteria. These demonstrations were quite theatrical and some of the so-called patients may in fact have been actresses and actors. Watching

Charcot's *tour de forces,* however, contributed to Freud's gradual move from anatomy to psychology, and eventually from the brain to the mind.

At Brucke's lab, Freud had met Joseph Breuer, a prominent Viennese internist with whom he began to actively collaborate after his return from Paris. As Freud describes it, they made a "chance observation" that if, under hypnosis, the patient recalled the memories of when the symptoms first occurred, the person's condition improved. This is what he wrote in 1893:

> "For we found, to our great surprise at first, that each individual hysterical symptom immediately and permanently disappeared when we had succeeded in bringing clearly to light the memory of the event by which it was provoked and in arousing its accompanying affect, and when the patient had described that event in the greatest possible detail and had put the affect into words". In other words the memory and the emotion related to it were repressed and by the help of hypnosis could be recalled or perhaps relived" (*S.E.* II: p. 6).

Freud and Breuer gradually went in different directions, most likely because of their differences in regards to the importance of sexuality in the development of hysterical symptoms. One of the consequences of their no longer collaborating was that over a brief interval of time, Freud decided to give up hypnosis and replace it by first just asking patients to see if they remembered what event preceded the appearance of the symptom. He observed a great deal of resistance to this request which he attributed to the force of the repression, and therefore came up with a technique to increase his pressure on the patient to recall the event. He had them lie down, close their eyes and remember, and when they couldn't, he put his hand on their forehead , press it, and suggested they tell him what appeared before their eyes. Over time he gave up on the pressure on the forehead part of his technique and just asked the patients to tell him what came to mind in regards to a specific symptom or event. This was the beginning of what was later to be known as free association, namely the psychoanalyst asking the patient to speak freely and say whatever came to mind without censoring.

The difficulty patients had in easily recalling or reporting on these events or memories led Freud to the notion of resistance, that is to say a force was preventing the pathogenic memory from being recalled. The memory was fended off or repressed, and a force kept it in that state and resisted it becoming conscious. From early on, he had noticed that such memories were often of a sexual nature, and this had led him to distinguish two sets of instincts, the sexual and the self-preservative or ego-instincts. Therefore, in 1915 he defined repression in this way: "The essence of repression is simply turning something away and keeping it at a distance, from the conscious" (*S.E.* XIV: p 147).

In other words, keeping something considered to be forbidden away from awareness. Until Freud began to focus also on aggression, and later on what he called the "death instinct," repression was primarily centered on the sexual instinct. Thus, sexual desires and wishes considered by the ego, originally meaning the person, and after 1923 referring to the executive function of the mind, to be unacceptable or forbidden had to be pushed out and kept out of consciousness, and that from this there would be a resistance to making them conscious. The dynamic unconscious, therefore, as opposed to regular so-called cognitive unconscious described above, was where all the repressed thoughts, fantasies, or desires resided or, put another way, they formed the dynamic unconscious.

Freud (1925) briefly stated it in this way: "The theories of resistance and of repression, of the unconscious, of the aetiological significance of sexual life and of the importance of infantile experiences—these form the principal constituents of the theoretical structure of psycho-analysis" (*S.E.* XX: p. 40).

Incidentally, this work of Freud entitled an "Autobiographical Study," is a good general introduction to his ideas which, by this point, 14 years before his death, were complete except for some additions later.

In his work "Inhibitions, Symptoms and Anxiety," published in 1926 and, in my view, one of his last comprehensive exposes of psychoanalysis, Freud summarizes and adds some modification to his notions of symptom-formation and the role of repression. In other words, he lays down how by 1926 he was using his psychoanalytic theory to explain symptoms, sources of anxiety, and inhibitions. The latter meaning that the person does not have an actual symptom but is unable to do certain things, such as being unable to form a sexual relationship.

But, before we can tackle this work we need to be clear in our minds about the anatomy of the mind or the psyche that Freud had described some nine years earlier in the work called *The Ego and the Id*, and which he had re-described in the *New Introductory Lectures,* under the title: "The Dissection of the Psychical Personality." Frustrated by the impossibility of describing his findings in neurophysiological terms, at the time thought to have been due to the fact that brain science was in its infancy, Freud chose to create his own functional entities of the mind. The Id represented the instincts which, for Freud, were the sexual or sometimes referred to as the *life* instinct, and the destructive or aggressive instinct which was also the *death* instinct (this latter concept, as I have indicated elsewhere, was not universally accepted by his followers), and finally, the Superego which is both a part of and independent from the ego, and which is the "conscience" with its self-observational (judging) property.

In "Inhibitions, Symptom and Anxiety", incidentally, one of my favorite papers of Freud, he attempts to clarify certain points about repression (which he clearly now defines as one defense amongst many, such as displacement or isolation, but a central one, though he alludes to the fact that different defenses may be more important in different pathologies) now explained through the lens of the tri-partite theory of the mind. When an "excitatory process" (p. 91) occurs in the Id, in other words when an instinct, sexual or aggressive, is activated, the ego succeeds in inhibiting or deflecting it with the use of the process of repression. Why and how does this occur? in the *New Introductory Lectures,* where he discusses in detail the relationship between Id, Ego, and Superego, he concludes that at the behest of the Superego, the Ego is able, by the process of repression, to keep an unacceptable or forbidden impulse that has been aroused in the Id from becoming conscious. However, analysis shows that the idea often persists as an unconscious formation. To put it simply, the person has an impulse which the ego or the superego does not approve of and, therefore, keeps it from coming into awareness and/or leading to enactment. Freud then asks what happens to the impulse, and he hypothesizes that the entire excitatory process in the Id does not occur at all because the Ego, through repression, succeeds in inhibiting it. How does the person know that there is such an impulse arising in the Id? Anxiety is aroused, the so-called signal anxiety informs the system that an instinctual impulse is about to be aroused, and the ego then employs repression to deal with it.

I am attempting to simplify what Freud actually wrote which is, at times, rife with contradictions and not always consistent from one page to the other. While on one hand he is trying to keep deepening and correcting problems, on the other he keeps piling on further complications. Psychoanalysts after him have tried in various ways to re-interpret or state in simpler terms his exposes, including Anna Freud in her book *The Ego and the Mechanisms of Defense.* They have questioned what is repressed: Is it the emotion? Is it the impulse? Is it the memory? And so on. Once one begins theorizing without clear and sufficient evidence, it is not too hard to get into all sorts of debates regarding small points. The fact remains, however, that even though Freud described other mechanisms of defense and others, specially Anna Freud added to it, for most of the life of psychoanalysis, repression has been seen as a central mechanism of defense, and responsible for symptom formation. A forbidden impulse is aroused, the ego tries to keep it under lock and key but in some cases it does not succeed, and a compromise is achieved in the form of a symptom. Incidentally, we should keep in mind that until relatively recently, neurosis was seen as a clear cut illness, and repression as one of the mechanisms that was involved in the understanding of the neurotic illnesses, and in their cure. In fact, as psychoanalytic theory evolved, especially in the United States, and many thinkers contributed to the theory, some refining it, some simplifying it, some using it to apply to literature, others to art, or to societal woes, repression kept its important role and became part of everyday parlance. At the New York Psychoanalytic Institute, therefore, many wrote about it and I will quote from a paper by Charles Brenner published in 1957. Charles Brenner, was probably one of the most prominent psychoanalysts from the 1960s until his death in 2008. He went to college at Harvard at 16, went to Harvard Medical School and, after a stint in neurology, went into psychiatry and psychoanalysis.

He chaired a monthly study group called the Kris Study Group named after its originator Ernst Kris. Kris, along with Heinz Hartman and Rudolph Lowenstein, all emigres from Europe, were part of a threesome that had a major theoretical impact on the thinking of those trained at NYPSI. Hartman was one of the key people who moved psychoanalysis in the U.S. from a focus on instincts and the Id to a focus on the Ego. The so-called "Ego Psychology" became the dominant school of thought in the U.S., and was much criticized in Europe, especially in France where it was considered to be superficial psychology. Far from it, Hartman's thinking was very sharp, complex, nuanced, and far from superficial, nor was the theory. Brenner belonged to the second generation of that school, along with Jacob Arlow,

David Beres, and Martin Wangh. Brenner and Arlow were, of the four, the most influential in New York and the U.S.A.

I joined the Kris Study Group as soon as I was allowed, which was in the third or fourth year of training, and was very much influenced by Brenner's clear and concise thinking. I had heard from him in medical school when an American friend had lent me Brenner's *Introduction to Psychoanalysis*, which was translated into many languages. I had found it enlightening but not as stimulating intellectually as what Professor Mertens de Wilmar was teaching. Nevertheless, I found the book a very useful introduction and enjoyed being part of the Study Group a few years later. Some time after that, I asked him if he would supervise one of my cases, which he agreed to do and, following that, I gradually became very good friends with him and his wife Irma, so much so that he wanted me to interview him for the archives of the New York Psychoanalytic Institute, which was, at that time, collecting interviews of our illustrious members for posterity. I also interviewed Nicholas Young, another powerful and influential member of NYPSI, but not prominent in terms of publications as Brenner. Nick was the guru of dreams when I was a student, and he eventually had me teach with him, and I later took over the dream courses.

Going back to Brenner's 1957 paper, incidentally, the lead paper in the important publication called *Psychoanalytic Study of the Child,* the idea for which came from Ernst Kris, and the particular issue featuring Brenner's lead article was in honor of Kris who was recently deceased at the relatively young age of 56. Brenner, divided the evolution of Freud's thinking on repression into four periods. The first from late 19th century when Freud and Breuer were collaborating and Freud was also still, to some degree, under the influence of Charcot at the Salpetriere in Paris, where he had spend a few months. As Brenner describes it, Freud observed, once he had given up on hypnosis, that patients resisted remembering what they were "urged or commanded" to reproduce. He then assumed that these memories were actively put out of consciousness, either when they had occurred or soon afterward. And again, as Brenner describes it, Freud concluded that such active suppression of memory, usually a painful or distressing one, was different than ordinary, unmotivated forgetting, and proposed to call it *repression*. As he saw more patients, and attempted to cure their neurosis, he came to, in his mind, the discovery which was to dominate the psychoanalytic world to this day, namely that hysteria, certain phobias, obsessional neurosis, and some paranoias were the result of pathogenic repressed memories persisting into adult life, and that if these memories were unearthed and carefully studied, they invariably led back to early experiences where the memory and the painful accompanying emotion (affect, as it is referred to in psychoanalytic literature) were repressed,, and that if these were traced back they led to childhood sexual experiences from around the ages of 8 to 10. Of note also, was his view that not only the memories were no longer conscious, since they had been repressed, but also that the mechanism by which they were pushed out and kept out of consciousness, namely repression, was similarly unconscious. In this period Freud ended up asserting two other important ideas: one, that since these early memories were sexual in nature, there was an infantile sexuality, and two, that the memories from childhood which were repressed had originally been a source of pleasure. Only at a later date, had they given rise to emotions of guilt, disgust, or shame, and therefore repressed. Again, as Brenner summarizes it, Freud then developed two other notions: the notion of the return of the repressed, which is essentially that if a symptom has to appear, the repressed must be attempting to become conscious, and the other idea that there is a battle between the push for the return of the repressed and the attempt to prevent it, leading to a compromise between the two forces—that is to say, the force of the memory and the forces that struggle to keep it repressed. This compromise is then essentially the neurotic symptom.

At the end of the paper Brenner describes Freud's final ideas and, to some degree, where things were at the time he wrote the paper in 1957. Here is what Brenner wrote summarizing Freud:

"Repression is one of several defense mechanisms which the ego may employ against an instinctual drive which is the source of anxiety. Thus the occasion or motive for repression is anxiety, usually anxiety aroused by a derivative of an instinctual drive. The target of repression is usually a libidinal drive, but it is possible that repression may also be employed against an aggressive or destructive drive and it may certainly be so employed against a superego demand."

Brenner himself, in the last years of his career, changed his view of repression and defense, and simplified all mental functioning as compromise formations. This is not the subject of the current work and I will leave that for others to evaluate.

Now we come to why I think the theory of repression presents serious problems, and why it contributes to my assertion that some of the foundational theories of Freud's should be discarded. This is not to say Freud's ideas did not also have a huge influence, to a large extent positive, on society, on our way of seeing the world and seeing each other, but that is a collateral though important benefit, and does not have directly to do with the validity of the main tenets.

Let us start with the "main well of the repressed," full of derivatives of instinctual drives, desires, and memories, which is the dynamic unconscious. Since the important contents of this unconscious are from childhood, the theory presupposes that from an early age the child has the ability to determine that some of her/his "sexual thoughts" are forbidden, and therefore dangerous, and he/she must keep them under lock and key. This assumes a knowledge in the child of what is sexual and what is not sexual, and what is prohibited and what is not. In other words, and this is true across most of Freud's work, it assumes a higher level of mental ability, more similar to an adult's cognitive ability than to what we know now to be the case during the early years of life. A child may have curiosities and even possibly sexual sensations (or what we as adults may assume to be sexual) but to think that he or she is aware of the forbidden nature of them to a degree that they need to be forcefully kept out of consciousness is not very likely, if not far-fetched. Related to the above is that in order to have this dynamic unconscious full of wishes, impulses, and memories that have to be opposed and thus kept actively and consistently out of awareness, some kind of force is assumed to exist (Freud also spoke of energy flow, which was an acceptable idea at that time given the paucity of knowledge about neuronal activity) that can keep these impulses or instinctual derivatives, by which he meant less direct manifestations of the drives (if indeed they exist), stored away so they don't become conscious. More precisely, it hypothesizes that there are two forces, one coming from the Ego or the Superego via the mechanism of defense, repression being our main interest for the moment, trying to keep the derivative (manifestation) of the instinct and the memory connected to it *out* of awareness, and another force, coming from the instinct, pushing for discharge. If the ego succeeds, the derivative is kept under control, if not, the ego may try to strike a compromise, and the result could be a symptom. There is no evidence whatsoever that such forces exist in the brain. In fact, neural functioning is infinitely more complex than what could be explained with a thermodynamic theory of physics. As I have already emphasized, given the primitive nature of knowledge about the brain at his time, people were just beginning to think about the transmission of electric currents along axons and the role of synapses, it is not surprising that Freud theorized with the knowledge of his time. The problem, however, is that his theories based on these early findings remained unquestioned until well past the middle of the 20th century.

But there are yet other problems with the theory of repression, and I will describe them below:

Creating a theory of repression based on the patient's resistance to reveal is a flawed thesis. The patient may simply be consciously withholding in order to avoid a painful emotion. In fact, it is clear from the early cases, and the need for the pressure on the forehead technique, that Freud employed prior to moving to the concept of free association, that he was really encouraging the patients to tell him what they had a hard time telling him, either because they were embarrassed, fearful, or just felt it was private, but which they *were* fully aware of. He was not lifting repression, he was lifting the conscious block to telling him their thoughts, wishes and fantasies. It is difficult to reveal your thoughts to a person you don't really know, even if you are convinced it is for your own good. Fear, shame, and embarrassment, even suspicion or lack of sufficient trust will work to keep one from just revealing one's private thoughts, fantasies, and wishes. Additionally, sometimes a certain memory or fantasy and thought may not be at the forefront of the mind, and may be recollected through an association with some other event or thought. This does not mean that prior to being recollected it was purposefully kept out of consciousness.

Furthermore, the original optimism of Freud and Breuer about the lifting of repression was not justified. The patients revealing their thoughts under hypnosis or pressure on the forehead did not show consistent improvement at all. Additionally, in a given situation what decides which part of a wish, memory, or experience is repressed? The entity Freud called the Ego, from early-on in his work, and which he later made, in part unconscious, is just a theoretical creation or invention and has no real existence.

While it is possible to talk of inhibition or even suppression in brain activity, it is difficult, as stated above, to justify the notion of force. Moreover, in developing the notion of cathexis (essentially the force associated with the wish, desire, and associated memory) and counter-cathexis (the force opposing the coming into awareness or even enactment of the wish, or desire, or the memory), Freud went even further out on the limb by asserting that these forces are not only involved in keeping ideas associated with instinctual impulses out of consciousness, but they are also involved in pushing them into consciousness. Given that the ideas are assumed to obtain their force by being associated to the instinctual impulse, then what is the source of the anti-cathexis? This issue was never comfortably resolved by Freud, and it does not correspond at all to what is presently known about brain function. In fact it can be said that the concept is based on a metaphor with no counterpart in reality.

Yet, another important problem is that the notion of repression implies discreet entities, be it a discreet memory or a specific wish. In the 1914 paper on "The Unconscious," Freud made the point that unconscious ideas, once submitted to repression, continue to nevertheless exist as actual structures in the system Unconscious. However, (as we know from memory research) wishes and memories are in constant interaction with other wishes and memories, this interaction moves both forwards and backwards, as present and past experiences influence and are influenced by other contents of the mind/brain creating networks. Therefore, there are no structures or discrete entities such as Freud delineated, rather, there are increasingly complex networks.

This notion of discrete entities is also problematic in relation to Freud's idea of the return of the repressed, which implies that one of these objects or discreet entities in the mind can enter consciousness in a circumscribed way and be recognized as such. Instead, we know that all experiences, including traumatic or emotionally relevant ones, are always present in the mind. They exist today because of the effect they have had on subsequent experiences; they are embedded in them. To the degree that any experience is in interaction with other past and future experiences, it is difficult to justify that recalling a specific event can alter all the subsequent effects of the original experience. I consider this a rather important point, most research is focused on the various types of memory and activities such as consolidation and re-consolidation, undoubtedly significant subjects of study, but as far as repression is concerned, the psychoanalytic interest has been on autobiographic memory and the therapeutic value of recovery of such memories of events. But, as mentioned earlier (chapter 5, p. 57), research has revealed that autobiographic memory is inaccurate, unreliable, and in parts created. Often, an event you may have heard about and imagined in your mind may get classified with similar events you have witnessed and, therefore, not recalled as if just imagined. In the past, I asserted, and rather forcefully, that such changes as may occur in a memory are tendentious—by which I meant that unconscious psychic conflict is the reason why memories are altered, not that it is a property of autobiographic memory and consolidation and re-consolidation. In fact, I believed that re-consolidation facilitated the tendentious alterations of memories, and that, through psychoanalysis, understanding the unconscious determinants of the alteration of memory was a path to discovering the unconscious conflicts leading to a more accurate picture of the past. I do not think so any longer. Though it is true that we do encounter situations where we can see that the memory alteration is tendentious, in those instances the motive is not hard to find, and often it is to protect us from feeling we have done something bad, shameful, or embarrassing—motives that do not reside deep in our unconscious, and do not relate to the childhood developmental conflicts that Freud described, not to say invented. However, if we take these neuroscientific findings into account, namely that most autobiographic memories are altered or even totally fabricated, as in false memories, then we have to accept that memories are at least partially an unreliable record of our past; they help us create a narrative of our lives but not one that accurately describes our trajectory. In other words, memories will not help the psychoanalyst fully understand his or her patient. This is why I have, to a point artificially, focused on experience. What do I mean? Let me give an illustration. Someone goes to a small town in India, Varanasi, for example, and lives there for 6 months (a place extremely unsimilar to where he or she is from). When she/he returns to his home in, let us say, New York, that person will have many memories to report on and, over time, these memories will change, and some will be forgotten, but the day-to-day experience of Varanasi is now part of who she/he is. The person back from six months in India is, in certain ways, different from the one who left six months before. A more powerful example is, of course, that of soldiers who have been to places of war; inevitably, their experiences changes them, and I am not even talking about PTSD where also it is not a few memories that are traumatic but the whole experience that continues to affect them in a powerful way. This has led me to propose, and it is how I practice: that understanding the experience of a patient, what kind of a life the person has had, especially in early life but not only, in large part through the patient's self-reflection as well as what we call the transference—that is to say how they see and experience us, the analysts—represents the key to understanding the issues of today for the patient. I may come back to refer to this proposal of mine again as I review the other main tenets of Freudian theory. If my assertions about memory versus experience are correct, then they would represent an important additional argument against the notion of repression. To repeat, the patient does not change or symptoms disappear, as Freud asserted, by the so-called lifting of repression and the uncovering of the traumatic memories, but rather the patient changes by looking at himself uncritically and for a long period of time, describing his experiences of others, of everyday life, and of the analyst. For example, if a person has lost a parent at a young age, it is not just the grief over the loss that matters but rather how their experience of everyday life was different when the parent was alive vs. when the parent was not. I have seen too many cases where the analyst takes every difficult event in the patient's current life and connects it to the patient's feelings of loss with no result whatsoever except, at most, a false narrative. The person would have been in certain ways different if the loss had not occurred, not only because of ongoing feelings of loss, but because everyday life changed and, therefore, she or he experienced a different one than if the loss had not occurred.

It is worth mentioning, for those interested in other points of view, that my dismissal of the central role of repression has been questioned by, for example, Simon Boag from the Department of Psychology at Macquarie University in Sydney, Australia, who suggests that the concept of "Inhibitory Processes" explains the neural basis of repression.

Finally, one last point which I think is key to the questioning of the role of repression in psychopathology is that if we assumed that repression is in fact a real phenomena—that is that the importance of repression in psychoanalysis lies in the idea that childhood sexual feelings are repressed—in other words, if repression is closely tied to the theory of childhood, then is childhood sexuality as Freud discussed it? This is the subject of the next chapter.

References

Brenner, C. (1957). The Nature and Development of the Concept of Repression in Freud's Writings. *Psychoanalytic Study of the Child.* XII:19–46.

Freud, A. (1966). *The Ego and the Mechanisms of Defense.* Madison, CT: IUP 1966.

Freud, S. (1893). On the Psychical Mechanism of Hysterical Phenomena: Preliminary Communication. *Standard Edition* II:6.

——— (1914). On the History of the Psychoanalytic Movement. *Standard Edition* XIV:16.

——— (1915a). Repression. *Standard Edition* XIV:147.

——— (1915b) "The Unconscious". Standard Edition Volume XIV:159–215.

——— (1925) An Autobiographical Study. *Standard Edition* XX:40.

——— (1926). Inhibitions, Symptoms and Anxiety. *Standard Edition* XX:87–174.

——— (1923). The Ego and Id. *Standard Edition* XIX:12–66.

——— (1933). New Introductory Lectures on Psychoanalysis. Dissection of the Personality. *Standard Edition* XXII:57–80

Furer, M., Nersesian, E., & Perri, C., Eds. (1998). *Controversies in Contemporary Psychoanalysis: Lectures from the Faculty of New York Psychoanalytic Institute.* Madison, CT: IUP, p. 58.

CHAPTER 9

Childhood Sexuality

All of Freudian psychoanalysis is based on the assumption that children have sexual desires and wishes, and that these are what give rise to the kind of conflicts that are responsible for adult character, neurosis, and suffering in general. Freud of course assumed that they were also responsible for more severe mental conditions, and that they could help us explain almost everything, by which I mean art, literature, society, history, and more.

How did Freud come up with this? He never analyzed children, he did work in a children's hospital before he developed psychoanalysis but that is not where his data came from. There are four main sources: one is from his own self-analysis, the other from the analysis of adult patients, the third one from existing ideas of the time about perversions, specifically those of the sexologist Krafft-Ebing. A colleague summarized very succinctly and correctly this source of ideas about childhood sexuality:" In the *Three Essays* the perversions became the prototypes for the mental life of childhood". The last one may be from the observations of little Hans by his father, under Freud's tutelage. Freud made it clear in the discussion of the little Hans case that what he learned in the case from the observations of Hans's father, under Freud's tutelage, confirmed his ideas presented in the *Three Essays on Sexuality*. So perhaps a more correct way to look at it is that he felt the case of this little boy confirmed his pre-existing hypothesis. As I have said already in one of the chapters, it is good to keep in mind that we are talking about an early period for modern science, a time that you looked for confirmation of your hypothesis, and if you found it then your hypothesis was correct. No need for peer review or double-blind studies. Confirmation bias was rampant among the scientists of the time who had no idea this bias was at work. The problem, of course, is that when a person comes up with an idea in the absence of a real challenge, the person believes in his/her idea, whether an insight, a discovery, or a theory. I mentioned this to Daniel Kahneman, and he disagreed, and even though I brought it up two or three times, he maintained his strong disagreement. Maybe he is right, after all, I am here believing in my own hypothesis. Nevertheless, just in case Kahneman is wrong, it is something one needs to be aware of all the time, and especially when one is in the business of telling people what they are really thinking, feeling, or reacting to, which is what we psychoanalysts do. But, enough of this diversion lets go back to Freud.

The Three Essays on the Theory of Sexuality is a foundational work in Freudian psychoanalysis, and I would like us to delve into it a bit and see what it contains. They were first published in 1905, therefore relatively early in Freud's journey, however, Freud kept enriching them and adding new sections for many years. In the introduction to these essays published in the collected works, James Strachey, the editor, says this about this work: "*The Three Essays on the Theory of Sexuality* stand, there can be no doubt, beside his *Interpretation of Dreams* as his most momentous and original contributions to human knowledge."

When I read this statement while working on this chapter, I was taken aback by this comment of Strachey's. The notion that the ideas presented in this work of Freud's were "a momentous contribution to human knowledge" suddenly, and unlike the previous times I had encountered such assertions, amazed me and I thought: How could we have had such grandiose ideas? We, because all psychoanalysts felt this way.

So, what is this momentous contribution? I think the simplest way to put it is that, unlike what was thought before, it asserted that children have sexual impulses which seek gratification. Other workers in the field had also started looking at the sexual nature of certain behaviors of children, amongst them Lindner and Moll. While disagreeing with their specific ideas, Freud nevertheless, mentions them to buttress his views of childhood sexuality. In fact, the period when Freud wrote the *Three Essays on Sexuality* was one of increased interest in the sexuality of children, and a beginning of normalizing some childhood behaviors, such as what was seen as masturbation which earlier was considered a sign of degeneracy. It can in fact be said that Freud, to a degree, helped parents accept certain behaviors in toddlers and little children, however, he also managed to give them a pathogenic significance.

As I have noted above the source of the data for Freud were his adult patients and Charcot, who had already stressed the importance of sexuality in Hysteria. But there was one problem in Freud's "basing my ideas (of childhood sexuality) on the examination of adults," and that was simply the fact that adults did not remember any sexual thoughts and activity from their childhood. To solve this dilemma and later consider it as proven, Freud hypothesized that the reason for not remembering was the phenomenon of "childhood amnesia."

This, is indeed ingenious because it allows the psychoanalyst to make assumptions about the patient's childhood based on the theory without actual need for confirmation from the patient. Let us take the famous oedipal complex which has become so much part of our culture that one does not need to be a trained psychoanalyst to attribute oedipal problems to people one knows. During all of my practice, and as I have said until the early 2000s, I was a committed classical analyst, I understood and communicated to my patients the oedipal meaning and reasons of their difficulties, such as guilt for wanting to kill your father to have your mother to yourself. Patients listened, some went ahead and ascribed to it some of their other problems, and yet no one ever said to me: "Yes, I remember I used to think this." Patients came to me who had been through a full analysis, and they would tell me, "I don't know why I still feel this way when I have fully analyzed my oedipal conflicts." Freud is the inventor of this complex, and once all the analysts around him accepted the idea, it was what they looked for, and child analysts, including Anna Freud, confirmed its validity. In reality, children rarely if ever actually expressed anything akin to oedipal wishes, and so a concept called "derivatives of oedipal conflicts" was invented to take care of the problem. Derivatives means the actual idea may not be conscious but related ideas that refer back through the psychoanalyst's interpretation to the unconscious idea provide proof of its existence. As I hope it is clear, the person who took the conscious thought of the patient and considered it to be a derivative of an unconscious sexual wish or conflict was the analyst. The phenomena of finding what you know you are going to find became scientific in psychoanalysis. Thus, after establishing that the reason adult patients and adults in general did not remember their childhood sexual impulses was due to childhood amnesia, the next task was to define what these impulses were. Here, Freud provided a theory beginning in early life.

The first objective evidence, to Freud, of what he considered childhood sexuality, was thumb sucking. Unlike others who had determined that such behavior in children was pathologic, Freud asserted, correctly, that it was part of development, though some children indulged in it much more than others. He attributed the need for thumb sucking to the search for a particular kind of pleasure, a pleasure that had started with the sucking of the mother's breast, and which he considered a sexual pleasure. Because the mother's breast, the primary erotogenic zone, is no longer available after weaning, the thumb becomes a secondary erotogenic zone albeit of an inferior kind. The thumb then gets later replaced by the lips of another. The character of erogenicity that here belong to the mouth and lips involved in the act of kissing, applies to other parts of the body, for example, the genital organs, however, Freud also believed that aside from the predetermined areas, lips, genitals, etc., any part of the body could assume the character of erotogenicity, and Freud, in a 1915 footnote to this section of the essays, wrote: "After further reflection and after taking other observations into account, I have been led to ascribe the quality of erotogenicity to all parts of the body and to all internal organs." This brief footnote of course is extremely important because it underlies the whole psychoanalytic explanations of psychosomatic disorders.

Freud started with the mouth, the oral zone, and hypothesized that this is where the sexual instinct arose from, and he regarded it as the first stage of development in the infant. He then moved to the anal zone, another locale from which the sexual instinct arose, and it now became the second stage in the psychological advancement of the child. What is the pleasure derived from the anal zone? This is how Freud presents it:

"Children who are making use of the susceptibility to erotogenic stimulation of the anal zone betray themselves by holding back their stool till its accumulation brings about violent muscular contractions and, as it passes through the anus, is able to produce powerful stimulation of the mucous membrane. In so doing, it must no doubt cause not only painful but also highly pleasurable sensations."

This second erotogenic zone was, over time, to become important in explaining other nervous disorders or neurosis, which I will describe later.

As the reader can imagine, the next bodily area Freud tackled was the genital zone: "Among the erotogenic zones that form part of the child's body, there is one which certainly does not play the opening part and which can not be the vehicle of the oldest sexual impulses but which is destined to great things in the future". Great things indeed, for castration anxiety and penis envy became foundational ideas for Freud, the latter not so much by most analysts in the 1980s or '90s, but certainly for a long time.

Another quote from Freud can help the reader appreciate Freud's thinking on the matter:

"The anatomical situation of this region, the secretions in which it is bathed, the washing and rubbing to which it is subjected in the course of a child's toilet, as well as accidental stimulation such as the movement of the intestinal worms in the case of girls, make it inevitable that the pleasurable feeling which this part of the body is capable of producing should be noticed by children even during their earliest infancy, and should give rise to a need for repetition."

Aside from what the sentence says about Freud's thinking on the matter (and you can almost say the data on which he is building is his own theory), it contains an important clue to the psychoanalytic view of pathology, namely that outside circumstances can intensify the pleasure and lead, for example, to pathologically excessive masturbation, that is to say, in the way the observation and hypothesis is structured, the path or roadmap to future pathology is already potentially traced. So, if the caretaker paid too much or too little attention to the child's genitals, it would have future consequences and effects. Thus it sets up, in a preliminary way, what is to become central in psychoanalytic theory of psychopathology, namely, that early life experiences (at the time of the writing of the *Three Essays,* primarily seduction by adults), can lead to symptom formation and adult disorders of the mind. It is in these same lines that Freud asserted the idea that a disposition to perversion of every kind is a general and fundamental human characteristic. By perversion he meant a deviation from direct sexual intercourse.

The distinction amongst the different erotogenic zones led Freud to describe the phases of sexual development, which is I imagine self evident, oral phase, anal phase and genital phase, and finally the oedipal phase. The oral phase, therefore pregenital, was also what Freud called cannibalistic pregenital sexual organization. He asserted that sexual activity had not yet been separated from their ingestion of food, and the sexual aim was the incorporation of food, which is the object at this time. Simply put, an adult thumb-sucker is revealing his/her attachment to this phase of development, just as a person with constipation is showing their fixation on the anal phase.

The consequences of the genital phase is, of course, the famous Oedipus Complex. The importance of this can not be minimized in Freud's theory. In a foot note on the third essay of the *Three Essays,* entitled "Transformations of Puberty," Freud said the following about this complex:

"It has justly been said that the oedipus complex is the nuclear complex of the neuroses, and constitutes the essential part of their content. It represents the peak of infantile sexuality, which, through its after-effects, exercises a decisive influence on the sexuality of adults. Every new arrival on this planet is faced by the task of mastering the Oedipus complex: anyone who fails to do so falls a victim to neurosis."

I should mention that the Oedipus Complex was also important because how it was resolved had a significant role in the development of the Superego. In fact, in our jargon we considered the Superego as the heir to the Oedipus complex.

Freud first used the term Oedipus in a letter to his close, if not closest, friend of the time, Wilhelm Fliess, on October 15, 1897. Fliess, a German ear-nose-and-throat specialist, was on a visit in Vienna to study with local specialists, when Joseph Breuer suggested that he attend Freud's lectures. Soon the two became friends, and in November 1887, Freud wrote his first letter to Fliess, which ignited a close friendship that lasted until late 1902. Freud and Fliess shared many of their ideas together through these letters, and through their meetings in person in various locations. These letters are a good source for anyone interested in following the development of Freud's ideas between 1888 and around 1900 when the friendship began to cool.

On October 1897, Freud wrote to Fliess: "I have found in my own case too, (the phenomenon of) being in love with my mother and jealous of my father, and now I consider it a universal event in early childhood, even if not so early as in children who have been made hysterical." And then: "…if this is so, we can understand the gripping power of Oedipus Rex, in spite of all the objections reason raises against the presupposition of fate, and we can understand why the later "drama of fate" was bound to fail so miserably."

By the way, Freud was involved at the time in his self-analysis which he did not find easy because of having to be totally honest with himself, which was to become the request for patients to say whatever came to their mind in the so called requirement of "free association" in psychoanalysis. Of interest also, is what has been noted by many, that Freud in a certain way used Fliess as the analyst who listens (in this case reads) his associations.

In the *International Dictionary of Psychoanalysis* which Alain Mijola, a French analyst, put together, and on which I worked quite intensely, reading every single entry and suggesting corrections both in subject matter and translation, for the American edition, under the Oedipus Complex, it states the following caveat: "Although very direct expressions of the Oedipus Complex can be observed in young children, for the most part, it manifests itself through unconscious formations identifiable only through their transposition onto other objects and their impact on other kinds of conflict." In other words, you don't hear children expressing these wishes because they are unconscious or are expressed through other manifestations.

There is one more notion of Freud's that plays an important role in children's, and later adult symptomatology or character traits, and that is "Primal Scene and Primal Scene Fantasies." This has to do with the ideas children have about what parents do in the bedroom, and the ideas they form if they accidentally witness sexual intercourse between the parents or two adults, and finally, also with not actually seeing but hearing the sounds of intercourse. Freud assumed that, in majority of instances, children interpret or see an aggressive element in the act, namely that the father is hurting the mother. These fantasies then give rise to certain symptoms and/or character traits in the adult as mentioned above.

It may be useful here to mention briefly the concept or principle of "psychic determinism" which assumes that all psychic thoughts and acts are pre-determined and stem from a series of underlying wishes which are mostly unconscious. It relies on the concept of psychic causality, whereby nothing happens by chance. The principle is important both for the rule of free association and the interpretation the psychoanalyst gives. The patient freely expresses thoughts, and the analyst then connects them and relates them to childhood wishes and conflicts. In other words, every thought of the analysand stems from an unconscious source and has a meaning that the analysand is not aware of. *The Three Essays* are, therefore, central to psychoanalytic thought because they describe the source of all human conflicts, and are behind their symptoms, character, and perversions. The patient's manifest thoughts, that is to say her/his utterances have a latent meaning, and the cleverer the analyst, the better he is able to read in the manifest associations, the unconscious or latent meaning of things. This is why for Freud the "Unconscious," that is the defended-against wishes, thoughts, or impulses, is timeless, which means the childhood conflicts are as active today as when they first formed. I no longer accept this formulation for reasons that I hope I have made clear and will continue to make so, but it is true that our life is a continuum, and the experiences of our life, from childhood on, are what have made us who we are. I will describe my view on this in more detail later.

The above generally summarizes the significant part of the foundational underpinnings of psychoanalysis. Childhood sexual conflicts, to which Freud later added conflicts over aggressive impulses, are at the basis of psychopathology, but are also part and parcel of normal development. Freud did not offer many clinical examples through his many papers.

There is a lot more that he and then his followers have written about on the subject of childhood sexuality and fantasies but it is not my aim to present a comprehensive expose of psychoanalytic theory, rather only to point out the most foundational ideas and then write and describe my reasons for moving away from them.

Are children curious? very much so and fortunately, but is this curiosity motivated primarily by sexual instinct? I don't believe there is any real evidence for that. The evidence that exists from work with adults, or with children, or with observational studies of children, are all an application of Freud's sexual theories to the observation. I think most would agree that children become curious about sex organs and whether that is because parents communicate a certain forbidenness about them or it is innate, I do not know, but yes, they are curious, but that is very far from assuming that they have sexual wishes towards their parents, or that in boys they want to eliminate their fathers in order to have their mother for themselves motivated by a sexual instinct. Children, both boys and girls, in the early years, very much want their mother to themselves and do not want anyone, father, sibling, or others, to interfere in their possession of the mother's attention, but is this sexual in nature?

As to children touching or foundling their genitals, to call it masturbation is, for me, very questionable, and requires a brief detour to discuss sexuality and masturbation.

I checked Wikipedia for a definition of human sexuality, this is what it said: "Human sexuality is the way people experience and express themselves sexually."

This, to me, explains nothing really, so I looked for other descriptions and definitions and found the following from the WHO:

"… a central aspect of being human throughout life encompasses sex, gender identities and roles, sexual orientation, eroticism, pleasure, intimacy and reproduction. Sexuality is experienced and expressed in thoughts, fantasies, desires, beliefs, attitudes, values, behaviours, practices, roles and relationships. While sexuality can include all of these dimensions, not all of them are always experienced or expressed. Sexuality is influenced by the interaction of biological, psychological, social, economic, political, cultural, legal, historical, religious and spiritual factors." *(WHO, 2006a).*

It appears to be difficult to define sexuality in a broad general sense, it can be defined hormonally, perhaps emotionally, even behaviorally, but otherwise it is hard to offer a concise definition though everyone knows what they mean about sexuality especially as it refers to them. The problem this poses is that when Freud considered thumb-sucking, or stool-withholding as evidence of sexuality, he did not define exactly what he meant, but it is safe to assume he meant in the way we all refer to it in the nonscientific mode. Is a child playing with its genitals masturbation? One can say well, it involves a genital organ, and the child seems to repeatedly engage in the behavior which, for Freud was evidence of an expression of the sexual drive, but how can we tell if what the child is feeling is sexual? Certainly, the hormonal levels are very low, and we don't hear phantasies from children resembling what we know to be sexual, so how could one know the child had a pleasure that is sexual? The point I am trying to make is that though the child playing with his genitals may find enjoyment in it, I would think mostly soothing, there is no way to assume it is akin to what an adolescent or adult feels in a state of arousal, sexual activity, and satisfaction with levels of hormones at much higher levels than in the first years of life. Of even a larger consequence is the assumption that such activity as we see in children is responsible or foretells adult sexual behavior, orientation, or even pathology. Therefore, it is not an exaggeration to say that the theory was created on little or no evidence but in such a compelling manner that it remained a central part of our understanding of psychopathology.

In the late seventies, at the Kris Study group (which I have mentioned above), we decided to take on the study of masochism, and we did that in monthly meetings for around four years. I then wrote the final report on it, and I will copy here a small section of that report, where it can be seen how we understood the problems of a particular analysand in light of our theory and the role the *Three Essays* played in that understanding:

"The patient felt to be one of the more profoundly masochistic patients we studied, had a history of repeated experiences with enemas and anal suppositories, anal masturbation from an early age, and stool withholding until the age of 10. In the transference, she was often withholding of both material and money, and her fantasies often centered around wishes to soil and mess, particularly in the analyst's office. While the analyst felt that most important as a determinant of the woman's later sado-masochism was the type and amount of struggle which went on between mother and child in the period from more or less one and a half years to age three, other group members disagreed, preferring to emphasize that while the lack of a healthy early relationship with the mother certainly was important to understand this patient, this factor in and of itself could not be said to be truly specific for the woman's later sado-masochisitc disturbance, as there was ample evidence for ongoing trauma, both during the oedipal stage and later adolescence. For those who held the latter view, the patient's oedipal struggles and intense penis envy were seen as being expressed in anal terms; thus for her, the most important underlying meaning of the stool was a penis—it was what she masturbated with, it was what she retained, it was what she had taken away from her, it was what she wished to acquire."

Did she have fantasies of this sort that became conscious during the analysis? The answer was no, but that was not considered a hindrance in understanding the difficulties of this patient because we had all decided early on during the deliberations, and I quote again from the same report:

"In regard to this matter, there was considerable discussion as to whether such a fantasy had to be 'unearthed' so to speak before it could be assumed to exist or whether an inference from repeated derivative expressions would in some cases suffice, given our knowledge of the functioning of the mind. In the end , we were in agreement that such inferences, judiciously drawn could be considered valid evidence."

The concept of psychic determinism I have described allowed us to make such a determination. The fact that no such fantasy was discovered, did not mean it did not exist because the patient's symptoms and associations to us revealed such unconscious fantasies. Looking back, our certainty continues to surprise me.

Freud, like others at that time, saw sexuality in much of psychology, and developed unverified theories that he and his followers continued to validate within the psychoanalytic groups. In other words, they kept finding what they thought they would find. This was reinforced by a powerful effect of "groupthink" which made it that we reinforced and confirmed each others findings.

Why are the hypothesis described in the *Three Essays on Sexuality* not valid any longer for me? As I have made reference to in an earlier chapter, the paper I was writing on Fetishism sent me to some of the sources in Freud, and it was the first time that I realized that there was not much actual clinical data. Of course, it took a couple more decades before I began to have more and more questions about Freud's assertions and re-read the Three Essays. I fully recognized at that point that Freud had used adult perversions, some from his practice, I assume, but a lot from the literature, and used them as a model to describe childhood sexuality without any data. The small amount of data from the case of little Hans was totally contaminated because he used his now developed theories to feed interpretations to Hans's father, and taught him to see the child's utterances from the lens of his theories.

It is an indication of the power of these hypothesis that for thirty years or more I relied on them in my work, argued in their favor in various meetings, taught them to students and supervisees, and wrote case reports relying on them. Hoping that I have made a cogent argument for the perspective I am presenting here, I would like to move next to the theory of instincts.

Before I do that however, I need to stress that much benefit has come from Freud's focus on childhood, specially through work done by his followers. For Freud, the role the parents had in the child's problems was limited to ways in which they may have effected the oral, anal, and oedipal stages of development. For example, if a boy lost his father at the age of four or five, he may develop symptoms at that age or later related to his guilt for having his wish of possessing his mother gratified. Fortunately, others looked at childhood more broadly, Winnicott, Mahler, and others who studied childhood spoke of the quality of mothering, the prominence of anxiety, and even of the role of education in helping or hindering a relatively normal development. As a result we have a better understanding of child development which, in turn, has helped in finding better child-rearing methods, and has made parents much more attuned to the child's experiences.

Unfortunately for many, especially the Freudians such as myself, for far too long the focus remained on the psycho-sexual theory of childhood which limited the scope of our work, thus missing a whole expanse of issues that could lead to a more comprehensive analysis and, as a result, a more life changing outcome.

REFERENCES

De Mijola, A. (2005). *International Dictionary of Psychoanalysis.* Thompson-Gale, p. 1183.

Freud, S. (1900). The Interpretation of Dreams. *Standard Edition,* Volume IV–V.

——— (1905). Three Essays on Sexuality. *Standard Edition,* Volume VII pp. 135–245.

——— (1909). A Phobia in a Five-Year-Old Boy. *Standard Edition,* Volume X pp. 5–149.

Lindner, S. (1879). Das Saugen an den Fingern, Lippen etc. bei den Kindern (Ludeln). *Jahrbuch für Kinderheilkunde,* 14:68–91.

Masson, J.M. (1985). *The Complete Letters of Sigmund Freud to Wilhelm Fliess 1887–1904.* Belknap Press of Harvard University Press. pp. 15–272.

CHAPTER 10

Instincts

The theory of instincts or drives (there are some definitional differences between the two, but in sum they are the same thing) is another pillar of psychoanalytic theory. Freud described two instincts: what he called the ego-instinct i.e., self-preservation and the sexual instinct, i.e., propagation of the species. Aggression was added afterwards, replacing the ego-instinct and, as I will describe later in this chapter, at some point the aggressive drive morphed into the "death instinct."

To try to place the beginnings of the notion of instinct in Freud's work, one needs to go back to a period relatively early in his career when he wrote a monograph that he never published at the time because of his dissatisfaction with it. Originally referred to as "Psychology for Neurologists," in his letter to Fliess, it became known as *Project for a Scientific Psychology*. He struggled mightily with this project, and a few times felt like giving it up, but on October 20, 1895, he wrote the following to Fliess:

"In the course of a busy night ... the barriers were suddenly raised, the veils fell away, and it was possible to see through from the details of the neuroses to the determinants of consciousness. Everything seemed to fit together, the gears were in mesh, the thing gave one the impression that it was really a machine and would soon run of itself. The three systems of neurons, the free and bound conditions of quantity, the primary and secondary processes, the main trend and the compromise trend of the nervous system, the

117

two biological rules of attention and defense, the indications of quality, reality and thought, the state of the psychosexual groups, the sexual determination of repression, and finally, the determinants of consciousness as a perceptual function—all this fitted together and stills fits together! Of course I can not contain my delight."

However, the project then disappeared from view until some fifty years later when it emerged along with some more letters to Fliess. But, according to Strachey, the ideas in it persisted, and eventually blossomed out into the theories of psychoanalysis. This is indeed correct, for the Project contains the seeds of much of Freud's later ideas. It is not an easy work to read and, in fact, as candidates at the institute, we were never assigned it in our readings; therefore I never looked at the work until some twenty years after graduation. The reason for my attempt to study the Project was that during the days I was involved in Neuro-psychoanalysis I heard some neuroscientists mention the work (along with another monograph Freud wrote on Aphasia) and some even tried to re-interpret a few of Freud's speculations using more current data. I found the work difficult, confusing, and not always coherent but, as Strachey's quote above indicates, it does contain seeds of later ideas, and certainly of instincts which, at this early stage, appear to have a relationship to Q. The notion of Q is not very clear in the Project but it seems to be connected to the amount or quantity of excitation, which in turn is connected to the notion of free or bound energy. Energy or force or excitation are precursors of the concept of psychic energy which come from instincts. I think the term drive better expresses Freud's concept because it connotes the idea that the drive has force or energy. That is to say that it can drive the person to act in order to satisfy a wish or desire. Freud assumed that an instinct, which he considered early on to be biological, has a psychical representative, and that the representative is made up of two elements; one is an idea or group of ideas, and the other is the energy that cathects it or them in order to push them forward, that is to say, towards satisfaction. Cathexis and cathecting are terms very much used in psychoanalysis which more or less mean the thing, idea or ideas is/are invested with energy, force, or power. This separation between the idea and the force or energy or *quota of affect* (another term that is used which connects the energy to emotion) of the representative of the instinct (such as a thought) is central to repression and other defenses where either the thought can be pushed out of consciousness or the force or power or energy of it is neutralized and thus rendered ineffective. In modern psychoanalytic writings, this dichotomy will be expressed as either the thought or fantasy can be repressed or that the emotion attached to it can be.

I realize that what I am describing is somewhat unclear if not confused and confusing, but unfortunately this is the nature of this part of the theory. Freud used the term quota of affect to indicate the power or force accompanying an idea and it becomes clear in psychoanalytic work over time that what it is referring to is, in an approximate way, emotion. In short and put simply, the aggressive instinct is behind the emotions of rage, violence, anger, and destruction, whereas the sexual instinct is behind the emotions of love, caring and sexual desire.

As I mentioned above, the first instinct (Freud used the term Trieb which can be described as drive or instinct) that Freud was mostly interested in was, of course, sexuality. For the purpose of this work, there is no need to go into what Freud originally called the ego-instincts which were in opposition to sexual-instincts, which he later dropped, especially once he had developed his tripartite theory of the mind.

I have described in the two chapters preceding this one, the important role sexuality had and has in the theory, and for a good many years it was conflicts around sexual wishes, fantasies, desires that were seen underpinning all sorts of mental conditions. Aggression made its appearance as an independent instinct in a fully descriptive way in 1920 within the concept of a death instinct. The original idea of sexuality was, of course, sexual pleasure, which is why the conscious sensation of pleasure was not separated from sexuality. Over the years, however, sexuality became a much broader concept, and through the energy it was supposed to contain, that is to say the libido, it became something that in a sublimated form—that is to say not purely physical sexual form—it could be invested in all sorts of things. For example, in art, music, relationships in general, and even everyday work etc.

Of great importance in regards to this instinct is, as I mentioned above, that the energy of it underlined the all important "Pleasure Principle."

This idea originated with the "Constancy Principle," which was already introduced in the Project, and which gradually assumed a position of central importance in psychoanalytic theory. Even though the idea was modified in *Beyond the Pleasure Principle*, with the introduction of the death instinct, the "Pleasure Principle" remained and remains important in psychoanalysis. For Freud, the principle had first to do with the accumulation of excitation that was perceived as unpleasant, and its discharge as pleasant. Some of his thinking was based on knowledge of sexual arousal as it leads to orgasm. He considered the state of arousal as un-pleasurable and as leading to a need for discharge in order to restore homeostasis, and he enlarged this observation to encompass the realm of mental functioning. Again, Freud started with an observation and transmuted it into a principle of mental functioning, in the process conflating observation with explanation leading to a broadly applicable general theory. Pleasure in orgasm can be consciously experienced and readily observed, but how does it follow that the mind is regulated by the need to balance pleasure and un-pleasure?

This U-shaped tube concept of pleasure/un-pleasure was very much part of 19th-century science, and it was further advanced in our field by Charles Brenner. But while homeostasis remains an important concept in physiology, to my mind it does not apply to pleasure and un-pleasure. As any clinician has observed, arousal in itself can be pleasurable and there are people who enjoy maintaining arousal for long periods of time because of the pleasure derived from this state. Tantric sexual practices being one example. Additionally, pleasure today is not a simple, unitary concept; there are many varieties of pleasure, complex interactions exist between pleasure and un-pleasure., and some pleasurable experiences may have no connection to un-pleasure. For example, the delight of listening to a piece of music or the joy of seeing a work of art cannot be logically connected to un-pleasure. Instead, like any affective phenomena, pleasure and un-pleasure are conscious, whereas any regulatory mechanism is an integral part of how the brain/mind works. In any case, the principle dominated psychoanalytic thinking until 1920, when Freud wrote *The Beyond the Pleasure Principle*. This is how he introduced this work:

> "In the theory of psychoanalysis we have no hesitation in assuming that the course taken by mental events is automatically regulated by the pleasure principle. We believe, that is to say, that the course of those events is invariably set in motion by an unpleasurable tension, and that it takes a direction such that its final outcome coincides with a lowering of that tension—that is, with an avoidance of unpleasure or a production of pleasure."

In the years during the first world war and after, the impact of trauma became a subject of interest for Freud, and he hypothesized that severe trauma broke a protective psychic shield that normally acts to modify or nullify the effect of various intense stimuli. In other words, with severe trauma the stimuli are of such force that the organisms protective shield is ruptured, and therefore, the pleasure/unpleasure principle rendered inactive. This gives rise to the uncontrollable repetition of the experience of the traumatic event in waking or in dreams, an observation that went counter to the universal applicability of the pleasure principle, hence the monograph *Beyond the Pleasure Principle.*

In this work, Freud is masterful in how he gradually presents his arguments and draws the reader to see his conclusions as a major inevitable discovery. There is a certain grandiosity in the way he universalizes his findings here; true, he always did that, but to say "… the aim of all life is death," (p. 38), as opposed to saying that the conclusion of all life is death, is not only unproven by him but is almost speaking as if he were a prophet. He further continues the sentence with: "… and looking backwards, that inanimate things existed before living ones."

The conclusion he drew was that there is a force for life but also one for death and he called it the "Death Instinct". It is also useful to note that Freud does not only speak of humans or his patients but of "organisms," that is, all living things, and when he asserts (p. 39) that "the organism wishes to die only in its own fashion," he attributes agency and even wish to fundamental biological phenomena. It would be as if one were to say the organism chose to go into meiosis or mitosis.

It is this death instinct (*Thanatos*) then that is responsible for the fact that traumas repeat themselves in dreams or in memory, contrary to what the pleasure principle would suggest. This repeating of painful events in life, and in the analytic treatment in the context of transference (which I will review later), is the "compulsion to repeat," and it is the death instinct that is determining it. Freud never gave up the notion of a death drive, and saw aggression or the destructive instinct as a part of the death drive which was turned outwards. In parenthesis, he used Thanatos to explain sadism and masochism. To summarize, Freud started with ego-instincts which he more or less gave up, and sexual instincts, and, over the years most of his attention was on the sexual, then he began, through observations of repetition in the mind of traumatic events, to describe an aggressive or destructive instinct which he theorized was a manifestation of the death instinct. There have been suggestions that the first world war, and/or the loss of his daughter, were the factors that led him to come up with the notion of a death instinct and the assertion that "the aim of all life is death."

If we were to discard Thanatos, as too theoretical and without any scientific merit to support it, the following quote from *The Ego and the Id*, section on "The Two Classes of Instincts" written in 1923, reveals clearly the lack of solid data in Freud's theorizing on this subject which comes across more as science fiction than science:

> "The ejection of the sexual substances in the sexual act corresponds in a sense to the separation of the soma and germ-plasm. This accounts for the likeness of the condition that follows complete sexual satisfaction to dying, and for the fact that death coincides with the act of copulation in some of the lower animals.
>
> These creatures die in the act of reproduction because, after eros has been eliminated through the process of satisfaction, the death instinct has a free hand for accomplishing its purposes."

We cannot do the same with the aggressive instinct or the sexual instinct, and while instinct may not be the correct way to view them, aggression and sexuality do exist.

After Freud, and especially in the U.S., the notion of the death instinct was dismissed and totally replaced by the dual instinct theory, sex and aggression, and the understanding of patients in analysis relied on understanding their sexual and aggressive fantasies and impulses and the various ways they defended against it and created compromises or inhibitions. Additionally, Hartman, and then Brenner, in disagreeing with the notion of Thanatos, asserted that the pleasure principle applied also to aggression, that is to say discharge of an aggressive impulse leads to pleasure and therefore dismissed the idea of "beyond the pleasure principle" and relied only on the "pleasure principle".

As I have indicated above, this later principle is based on an understanding of the functioning of the mind in a hydraulic mode, that is to say, if a drive is discharged, it releases pleasure, and if it accumulates, it causes distress. A "U tube" model based on the flow of hypothetical energies. The other problem with the dual instinct theory is that it places all of human behavior under the aegis of these two drives. Therefore, all the activities of humans (and animals?) must and can be understood as either an expression of sexuality or aggression or both. Furthermore, emotions, which I have mentioned above, remain to this day somewhat elusive as to how well we understand them; in the Freudian model, they belong to these two instincts and polarities: pleasure or pleasurable and unpleasure or unpleasurable. Simultaneously, other activities needed for survival fall under these two instincts. A Freudian would say, hunger is both sexual and aggressive (involves chewing) and therefore, pathologies involving hunger (such as anorexia nervosa) would be understood as manifestations of sexual and aggressive conflicts.

For the purpose of this work, the question is what is wrong with this model?

First and foremost, I would say human behavior and emotions are too complex to be ascribed to these two drives. For example thirst, which we need in order to search for water, or making sure we have heat so we don't freeze in very cold weather. Humans (and animals) do many things for survival that have nothing to do with sexuality or aggression (we need to think better here and create a cohesive presentation, bringing in hormones, emotions, Ledoux' regulatory circuits, affection, anger as a consequence of anxiety, etc.). They eat, they hydrate, they thermoregulate, etc. Joseph Ledoux has used the term survival circuits for these circuits that lead to behavior in the service of survival. Second, it is assumed in Freudian theory that there can be unconscious aggressive feelings or unconscious sexual desire; in order to justify these you need to assume that there is such a thing as an unconscious state for emotions. I think there is a state where the circuits leading to emotion are not activated but in view of what an emotion is, it can not be unconscious. There is no desire until you feel a desire, no fear until you feel a fear and no anger until you feel it. There are degrees of desire or anger or fear but they can not be unconscious.

Therefore, the premise that analyzing repressed sexual or aggressive desires, or analyzing the compromises ensuing from these repressions, can lead to symptom change or psychological improvement does not have a scientific basis. Furthermore, as I have repeated many times, the whole idea of the flow of energy in these instincts which can be blocked, displaced, or released, and which is reliant on an energy model that Freud tried to tackle in the "Project for a Scientific Psychology," but which he did not pursue as a complete work, nevertheless maintaining the notion of forces called drives or instincts namely, eros and Thanatos, does not work.

REFERENCES

Freud S. (1895). Project of a Scientific Psychology. *Standard Edition,* Volume I: pp. 295–397.

———— (1920). Beyond the Pleasure Principle. *Standard Edition,* Volume XVIII: pp. 38–39.

Ledoux J. (2012). Rethinking the emotional brain. *Neuron* 73(4):653–76.

Moussaief Masson J. (1985). The Complete Letters of Sigmund Freud to Wilhelm Fliess 1887–1904. Belknap Press of Harvard University Press, pp. 15–272.

CHAPTER 11

The Problem of Violence in Humans

Thanksgiving 2018, while in Paris, I went to see an exhibition of Joan Miro at the Grand Palais. While I frequently go to art exhibits, I am not a professional, yet this exhibition struck me as particularly well curated and therefore instructive. As my wife and I were looking, we saw these three large impressive canvasses with strong lines curving in the middle, black lines, and three blotches of color, one red, one blue, and one yellow. Not being an artist or a critic, it is hard for me to describe it but though simple and minimal, it conveyed to me an undeniable sense of despair, emptiness, yet power. Upon looking at the title I was surprised to read "The Hope of a Condemned Man" painted in 1974. The description identified the condemned man as Salvador Puig Antich.

It is perhaps a coincidence but from the time I left Tehran in 1960, at every place I have pursued a segment of my education, I have quickly become very good friends with one person. In boarding school it was a Persian boy, "Firouz," and later a Yorkshire boy called "Tom," in Leeds College it was a Nigerian "Innocent," in Louvain an American "Joel," and a bit later a Belgian "Benoit," in Hotel *Dieu de Montreal,* "Marcel" at Hillside Hospital, "Steve," at Payne Whitney Clinic, "Tony," and at the New York Psychoanalytic Institute "Joachim." I don't know how it happens but it seems two people almost immediately find some common terrain and a friendship begins very quickly. Of course, some of the friends were foreigners like myself, but not all. Tom was English, Benoit was Belgian, and Marcel French Canadian.

Joachim and I were both active students in class at the institute. And so, when we made comments in class we were often in agreement on how we understood the papers or chapters we had read, and/or perhaps what bonded us importantly, was that we were both non-New Yorkers. He was from Spain though he had spent time in Paris. His last name was Puig Antich.

I remember when he told me about the tremendous fear and desperation, and mostly hopelessness he was feeling in 1974, because his younger brother had been arrested on wrong charges of having killed a policeman and was awaiting trial. While he knew his brother was an anti-Franco, as was he, and that he had been involved in some altercation with the government forces, he was sure based on what he knew from his parents and sisters who were in Barcelona that he, Salvador was innocent. The months until Salvador was executed, when we met at the institute three times a week, we could feel, along with Joachim, the up and downs of hope and despair. Many governments, worldwide, called for a stay of execution and when the Pope intervened, we felt a great sense of hope, but at the end, to no avail, a 25–26 year old young man was murdered in the most vicious way, garroted. The last person to be garroted in Spain by Franco's government.

Miro's painting brought back for an instant all the emotions that had been dormant for 45 years. Not just the emotions connected to this horrendous act of human barbarity but also following it about Joachim, whom we called Kim for short. After finishing the institute Kim moved to Philadelphia where he became a Professor of Child Psychiatry, and became famous for being one of the early people recommending psychiatric medication use in children, which at the time, I did not approve. Then tragedy hit again, this time in the form of an attack of "status asthmaticus," an unrelenting acute asthmatic attack that killed him. A painful death when you cannot breathe.

Remembering Kim and his brother's execution, underscored the feelings and thoughts I have been having for the past few years. Obviously, I have always been aware of the atrocities committed by humans on humans. Nevertheless, when president Trump was elected I was dumbfounded by the rage and aggression I had a chance to observe in my office and, of course, in the nation. People expressed fantasies of violent revenge on friends who they found out had voted for Mr. Trump; others listened to the news and became furious and agitated and enraged, some woke up in the middle of the night to check the news. Others wished all sorts of bad things happening to the President and the people in his cabinet. Suddenly, half the country were enemies; a person who had voted for Mr. Trump was considered the worst kind of person, the sense that we are all humans and share this world and this opportunity for life together disappeared. I began to deeply understand, rather than just know theoretically, that it is actually possible to agitate people enough to commit genocide. Trump supporters, with some added inciting, would become like (and I am exaggerating to make a point) the Armenians that the Turks killed, and the Jews that the Germans and others killed, and, of course, equally vice versa for Trump opposers. The situation brought to my mind that perhaps a major effort needs to go towards understanding the roots of aggression, not only in the super extreme cases but all cases. What lies behind this kind of rage where other feelings such as empathy, understanding differences of opinion, taking a balanced view, or hope disappear? I could no longer watch the news, the rage and the pleasure of the others' defeat, from each camp, was mind boggling. Then came Covid-19 which very rapidly led to many deaths, confinements, quarantines, closings of schools and universities, severe restrictions of travel, and entertainment, including going to restaurants, concerts, theatre, opera, and so on, and of course, the oft-repeated injunction: "wear a mask and keep social distance." Large swaths of the population in New York City, which is where I live and therefore observed most clearly, became very frightened. Those fortunate to have second homes outside the city left, and the rest stayed in their apartments except to go out to buy food or exercise. Supermarkets started having long waiting lines, and some products such as sanitizers, toilet paper, bottled water, flour, and other necessities became in short supply. In the middle of the pandemic a policeman murdered a black man by choking him with his knee on his neck. A horrendous crime, and now demonstrations began with good intent and the hope of eliminating the unfair, and in this case illegal, treatment of citizens of the black community. "Black Lives Matter" became an important slogan and, as I said, mass demonstrations took place in most parts of the country. What happened in almost every one of these demonstrations, however, was that a small group of violent men and women broke shop windows, set cars on fire and even harmed people. The rage became almost scary. The violence was on both sides of the political parties, and it seemed the smallest event set up another fire. The issue of a president holding back on appointing a Supreme Court Justice during the last months of his presidency had come up before, but this time when Justice Ruth Ginsburg, very beloved by the nation, died, and the president and the head of the senate spoke about nominating someone to replace her less than two months before the election, demonstrators even surrounded the home of the head of the senate, and they were threats of setting fires. Rage was palpable. I am on the listserv of the New York Psychoanalytic and the American Psychoanalytic Association. Rage became manifest in these listservs also, with members coming close to, if not insulting one another, and acting as if they were dealing with bitter enemies. In the NYPSI case a poorly expressed idea by a senior, mild mannered, kind member set up the fire and in the APsA case the elections was the trigger.

Sitting on the sidelines I was flabbergasted by the absence of all manners, decorum, respect and a certain gravitas which had always been part and parcel of the psychoanalytic world. Remember my description of anonymity, abstinence and neutrality. The outburst of anger, rage was in the psychoanalytic community as it was everywhere else. It was like the fires that were raging in California at the same time.

So what is responsible for this kind of aggression? I don't know but would like to offer an idea I have had to explain some of it. From the outset I should stress that this is just an idea, and I make no claim about its accuracy. My idea, speculative of course, is that some of the aggression we see is based on fear. Fear is what alerts us to protect ourselves against danger and at times that protection is through aggression. Freud did not see it this way, he believed in the presence of a drive or instinct which he and the followers called the aggressive drive. It is, in fact, in Freudian psychopathology, what can give rise to anxiety and fear. My idea turns it around and can help explain at least a certain number of relatively understandable events where a lot of anger and aggression is expressed. Does it explain cold-blooded murder not committed out of self-defense, or genocide? No, not really. Of course, you could unleash aggression or anger by claims of danger, and danger is a rather broad term in the current context; instability, threat to one's values, threat to established systems, as well as the kind of threats that lead to war, all give rise to fear and anxiety. But, there is a big step to take, between being threatened, sensing danger, feeling fear, and actually killing another human being: Someone who hears, sees, and feels just like us, who has loved ones, who is as attached to this short time on earth like we all are. You can metaphorically stab someone in the back, out of rivalry, greed, or ambition, but taking away the life of someone just like yourself, that I think, is something worthy of research across many fields: neuroscience, social psychology, and anthropology, and urgently. I remember the first time my wife and I went to *Siem Reap*, Cambodia. Naturally, going to Siem Reap was to see *Angkor Wat* and the other Wats, and so, on our second morning there, after visiting it on our own the day before, we hired a guide. He met us at the hotel, a tall, intelligent man in his forties, and began telling us about how Angkor Wat was discovered and all the kinds of information he thought tourists would like to know. At some point during the visit, we were at this tall set of stairs, and one could walk up and have a view of the vista all around. I decided to walk up but my wife chose to remain below with the guide. When I came down, they were sitting on the stone wall, and he seemed to be telling her about something that clearly was highly emotional. He was talking about the civil war and the torture and killings by Pol Pots forces, and how they had to hide in small underground dugouts. My wife was visibly touched and so was I when I heard the tail end of his family history. What makes men do this, the Nazis, the Turks, the *Khemer Rouge,* Nigerian forces against the Biafran civilians, beating, torturing, raping, mutilating and killing?

If the flight-or-fight response, i.e., fear as a trigger for fight does not explain these extreme kinds of aggression, what does?

Freud of course, had ideas about aggression, and in his famous letter to Einstein, published under the title "Why War," he elaborated the role of the aggressive instinct. By 1932, when he wrote the letter, he had gone beyond the concept that two instincts dominate our life: the erotic and the aggressive. He had speculated on the presence of an instinct in us which would explain the lust for destructiveness which he called the "Death Instinct". He originally described it in a paper entitled "Beyond the Pleasure Principle" (1920). In the letter to Einstein, this is what he had to say about it:

"As a result of a little speculation, we have come to suppose that this instinct (the destructive instinct) is at work in every living creature. And is striving to bring it to ruin and to reduce life to its original condition of inanimate matter. The death instinct turns into the destructive instinct when, with the help of special organs, it is directed outwards, on to objects. The organism preserves its own life, so to say, by destroying an extraneous one. Some portion of the death instinct, however, remains operative within the organism, and we have sought to trace quite a number of normal and pathological phenomena to this internalization of the destructive instinct."

This was a controversial idea, even within psychoanalytic schools, though in certain countries and within certain schools of psychoanalytic thought it remained a powerful explanatory tool. It was very much used by both Kleinian psychoanalysts (followers of Melanie Klein) and Lacanian analysts (followers of Jacques Lacan).

To me, the issue we are dealing with in everyday life, and which has never left us alone throughout the history of man, is the constant presence of aggression, in all its varied forms, including torture and murder. It is interesting to note that Freud, in the quote above, appears to imply that we protect ourselves by destroying another person; thus, he could be seen as saying that to protect ourselves we need the destructive instinct, which is, in a different way, what I have come to recognize. When we are frightened, our aggression is mobilized to protect us in case the danger reveals itself to be real or, unfortunately, even if it appears to be a possibility since we cannot take the risk of ignoring even a potential threat. Of course, when it becomes a matter of possibility versus certainty, then people can be led to feel more fear and, therefore, more aggression. There is no justification for either, but it cannot be eliminated and, through fear-mongering, people can be induced to commit horrendous crimes. Is there a way to change this progression in behavior which is to induce fear, activate aggression, and achieve destructive aims? Research on the subject is so scant, it is hard to tell if there will ever be a way to at least mitigate it in the civilized human. Perhaps understanding fully the neurobiology of it under various scenarios will help. This, if one is optimistic, could perhaps lead to methods, whether through early education, parental influence, or even genetic modification that could get us to a time where there will be no war, no murder, no killing.

References

Freud, S. (1920) beyond the pleasure principle. *Standard Edition* Volume XVIII: pp. 38–41.

——— (1932). why war? *Standard Edition* Volume XXII: pp.195–215.

CHAPTER 12

Interpretation of Dreams

In two volumes of almost 700 pages, Freud tackling and succeeding to unravel the secret of dreams would be considered a major achievement, except that he went much further; in those two volumes he explained how the human mind works. Without a question for every psychoanalyst, *The Interpretation of Dreams* is, along with the *Three Essays on Sexuality,* the skeleton on which the rest of psychoanalysis is built. It is, without a doubt, whether one agrees with the theories or not, a brilliant work.

When I was a student at NYPSI, the dream course, taught in the first year, was, just by its length, a full year, considered the most important course. Nicholas Young, a powerful figure at the institute, had been the person in charge of the course, having taken it over from Otto Isakower, also a highly revered member of the institute, but who had passed away by the time I began my training. Young was the head of the Education Committee which meant he essentially ran the institute and did so with an iron fist. When I took the course, it was taught by a very careful thinker, William Grossman, who had followed Young as the instructor. There was, however, a second course in dreams, given during the last year of training, as opposed to the first course given in the first year. It was a clinical course and it dealt with how to understand and interpret dreams, as opposed to understanding the way the mind works by studying dreams which was the *raison d'etre* of the first year course. Nicholas Young taught the fourth-year course when I was a candidate. Some time after I graduated, Young asked me to be his assistant teacher, and I did that for a few years, until I was assigned to teach the course on character. A few years after that, the instructor of the first-year dream course took Young's fourth-year clinical class as Nick did not want to teach any longer, and I was given that teaching assignment. I, therefore, had to re-read the whole two volumes many times during these years and, despite that continued to struggle with what was well known amongst psychoanalysts: "chapter seven of the dream book." Some years later, I moved from the first-year course to teaching the fourth-year clinical course, and did that for more than ten years. Additionally, I was in two study groups, one with Young in charge, and another with a group of senior colleagues, both on dreams.

What did strike me about Young's approach to dreams, and he had been the assistant teacher to Isakower, the guru of work with dreams, was that he did not seem to apply any theory, such as those in the *Three Essays,* namely pre-oedipal, oedipal, or latency ideas, to the way he described his understanding of a patient's dream, rather, he just spoke about capturing where a dream fell in the continuity of the patient's life. Not in the continuity of the patient's association, but the continuity of daily life. To him, it was not that the dream revealed a childhood conflict in need of being interpreted and made conscious but rather, that the dream revealed some interruption in the patient's mind, some point of resistance to the free flow of her/his thoughts that interpreting it allowed the associations to resume. I believe Nick's approach influenced me in my thinking about dreams over the years, and perhaps contributed to my current position which is not to see dreams as the great revelator of deep unconscious conflicts of sexual or aggressive nature.

Nick was an important figure in my early analytic life and remained so until his death. Our families became close friends and we had many good times together. Nick was born in Romania near the border with Hungary. He left for his studies to Switzerland at around age 16, where he went to medical school. Soon after graduating, a professor advised him to leave the country as the situation was becoming increasingly tenuous for Jews. Nick managed to secure a seat on a train to Spain, and there he remained for some time, waiting to get on a boat. He enjoyed himself in Spain and became a lover of bullfights, which he managed to go to for years afterwards during his summer vacations. He could not go directly to the United States, though that was his goal, but first ended up in Cuba where he spent two years before coming to New York City. While on the boat, he met an attractive woman whom he married but who turned out to be an alcoholic, and she died not many years into the marriage. While still married, he and his wife moved to New York where he eventually secured a residency in Psychiatry for himself, and then began psychoanalytic training. In the period he trained, there was no real organized training yet, but he did have to take some classes, have an analysis, and start seeing patients. He graduated in three years and managed to move up the ranks pretty rapidly. It is during this early period of poorly systematized curriculum that Otto Isakower, as head of the committee, established the first fully organized teaching program. This must have been in the late forties to early fifties, and the curriculum remained the same until I was put in charge of a subcommittee that I had suggested, to look and make changes to the teaching program. After consultations with many of the instructors, and talking to other institutes around the country, we revised the curriculum in a moderately drastic fashion and, importantly, managed to get the vote of the Education Committee, after much fierce debate and opposition. I think it was forty years after Isakower had organized the first one. The pace of change was no doubt slow.

Before going back to Freud, I must stress that the pace of change was extremely slow at the institute in those days, and every proposal was met with stiff resistance and hours and hours of debate. Today, the changes that would have taken years to bring about, if ever, have been happening with tremendous ease and at very rapid rate. Survival of psychoanalytic institutes was not the issue then, survival and protection of the purity of Freud and his early follower's thoughts was the goal and the duty.

Going back to *The Interpretation of Dreams*, the two most read chapters, in addition to where Freud discusses the famous "Irma's injection dream," are chapter six and chapter seven. Six because it describes the dream work—that is to say that the mechanisms that go into creating the finished dream we remember, and chapter seven is really an early sketch of Freud's theory of the mind. The first part of the book begins with a long review of the prevailing notions about dreams at the time, and it is some 98 pages long. Freud uses that section to debunk some ideas and to use others as a jumping point for his theory. In a recent book by Antonio Zadra and Robert Stickgold titled *When Brains Dream,* the authors claim and discuss the work of other individuals who had studied and written about dreams, and whose ideas preceded Freud's. Their claim is that Freud does not mention them, yet uses their findings.

There then follows the famous specimen dream, often referred to as "Irma's Dream," which takes one directly into Freud's thinking about dreams, and which is a good place to begin teaching dream interpretation. So what *is* Freud's theory of dreams? Freud saw the dream as the protector of sleep. This is where the whole idea of a dream expressing a wish as fulfilled originates. He observed that when he had had anchovies and olives for dinner, he would dream about drinking a big glass of water. Therefore, the wish to quelch his thirst was presented as fulfilled in the dream. Additionally, the dream in this way would make it possible for him to continue to sleep, the dream, in other words, would protect his sleep and allow him to sleep some more, unless and if the thirst was so intense that waking could not be prevented. From this finding Freud moved on to trying to understand other ways the dream is a protector of sleep and a presenter of wishes as fulfilled. He decided, based on his self-analysis and the analysis of patients, that other wishes could be presented as fulfilled, even wishes that may be prohibited from entering consciousness during waking, mainly sexual originally, and sexual or aggressive or both, later on. He proposed that during sleep a number of our ego defenses are lowered, including such things as logical thinking, and therefore, the repressed impulses seeking fulfillment are freer to enter consciousness. Since, the ego has to prevent these forbidden thoughts and desires from entering consciousness fully and waking the sleeping person up, it uses a variety of mechanisms to disguise the true meaning of these forbidden impulses, and represents them, nevertheless, as fulfilled, in order to prolong sleep. Dreams, however, are often illogical or represent things that would be impossible in real life; they don't seem to pay attention to time and place; dead people can appear as alive and vice versa; a person can appear in a dream as a combination of two people, for example, the head of a man and the body of a woman, and so on. This led Freud to make a distinction between waking thoughts which he called secondary process, and the thinking in dreams which he called primary process. The thinking in dreams, Freud asserted, is how thinking is in the unconscious, whereas conscious thinking is logical, that is to say that it belongs to the secondary process. This distinction between the conscious and the unconscious is how Freud had described the structure of the mind prior to 1923. I have described this model, called the Topographic model in an earlier chapter. It is good to keep in mind that the foundational parts of the theory of dreams is based on this model, and was then revised when the tri-partite model of the mind became the prevailing theory. Of course, as stated in the earlier chapter, Freud never abandoned the concept of the unconscious, it is just that it no longer was seen as part of the topography of the mind but as more a functional characteristic. Another important distinction is between what are called the latent dream thoughts and the manifest dream thoughts. The latter is the dream as the patient reports it, or as one remembers it; the latent is what the psychoanalyst interprets; that is to say it is the true meaning or intention of the dream. To reiterate, a dream, according to Freud, is the result of a repressed childhood impulse being activated, either by something that happened during the day before the dream, or became instigated on its own. This aroused impulse can, therefore, disturb sleep and, to prevent that, a hallucination occurs which represents the impulse as gratified, and thus allows for the sleep to continue. However, this gratified impulse has to be disguised, and the disguise is the task of the dream work which turns the latent dream thoughts (the hallucinatory wish fulfillment) into the manifest dream which then undergoes a secondary revision in order to give it a certain coherence present in the reported dream. Therefore, in dream analysis, the manifest dream thoughts, i.e., the dream as remembered and reported, is converted into the latent dream thoughts through the patient's associations. In other words, the patient says what the dream brings to mind and, together with the analyst, they reconstruct the latent dream thoughts which are the true meaning of the dream.

I have, in previous chapters, attempted to show the major flaws in the Freudian construct of the mind and, as I have indicated, I consider a good part of it simply unsupported speculation and frankly wrong. I feel just a bit different about dreams, however. While I think much of the theory does not hold, in working with patients, I have found dreams can help us and the patients understand what may have disturbed the patient during the day, and how that may relate to other issues, sometimes of importance, and thus get a better appreciation of what they find disturbing or problematic in their lives.

I think there is increasing evidence that sleep is important both to re-set the brain thermostat in terms of energy consumption, and to store and perhaps classify the memories of the day. What role, then, does the dream play? My own unverified theory, since I am not a neuroscientist and don't do research, is that one of the triggers for a dream's occurring is when it is difficult to easily sort out a memory or experience. An unexpected, unusual, or disturbing event, or something that was dissonant in an interaction, for example, interferes with the easy selection and storage of memories. A dream is the attempt at finding an explanation that would then allow the storage of that particular experience to occur and for sleep to continue, since I still think that Freud was right in believing that one role of dreaming was to protect sleep.

I remember having dinner with a couple friend of ours whom I had great affection, respect, and admiration for, and they seemed to have similarly nice feelings towards us. During the dinner, a subject came up which, in a very round-about way, put a less shiny light on their son. The father, in response to a benign comment of mine, made a rather sharp comment, totally uncharacteristic of him. Though I no longer remember my dream that night, in the morning, thinking about it, I realized it had to do with my utter surprise at his comment and the slight aggressive edge in his tone. It is then that I hypothesized that, perhaps, because I could not fit this behavior of the father into the same store of memories I already had of him in my mind, I had the dream that reflected this difficulty. In other words, the dream was the attempt by my sleeping mind to solve the incongruency. To repeat, my previous experiences with this person, more specifically my emotional experiences with him, and the comment of that night, were too asynchronous to be filed away in the same bank of my memories and experiences with him from the past. I emphasize emotional experiences, because emotions play a major role in our dreams. In fact certain juxtapositions in the dream that may seem incongruent, unrelated, or illogical, can easily be understood when the shared underlying emotion is recognized or discovered during the analytic work.

Again, it may be pure fantasy, but in my work, I do find insights about the patient when I look at the dream in this way.

I should add, however, that these hard-to-store events are not the only determinants of dreaming. Disturbing events from the day, especially if they relate to other past disturbing events, may also give rise to a dream.

As previously mentioned, I taught the two dream courses for a large chunk of my career at the institute, but then, some time around 2013 or

2014, I stopped teaching. I stopped because I had been teaching a long time, but at the institute, even 80-year-olds run for office or teach; the stronger reason was my dissatisfaction with the classes. We, myself and my assistant teacher, either had a couple of students in a class, or they added psychology interns to increase the size of it, but ones who had no experience whatsoever with psychoanalysis. Keep in mind the class, as it was taught, was traditionally a class for psychoanalytic candidates, given during the last six months of their training. In fact, for years if the candidate, for one reason or another, did not have a case in analysis, she or he was not allowed to take the class.

So it was with sadness that I stopped, not sad because I would miss teaching, but sad because I was seeing the end of psychoanalysis.

REFERENCE

Freud, S. (1900–1901). The Interpretation of Dreams. *Standard Edition,* Volume IV–V.

CHAPTER 13

Other Works of "Freud"

I have, in the last four chapters, covered what I consider to be the main arguments against Freud's theories. There are, however, a few additional things that should be mentioned in a briefer form to cover a broader spectrum of his work. But first I should say a word about the few cases Freud published of his work. These are of the patients he saw, such as Dora, the so-called "Rat man," the "Wolf Man," and a few examples from patients such as the famous "Irma Dream." He also published a work on "Schreber" but he never actually saw that patient. I have already mentioned "Little Hans" in an earlier chapter. These cases served to justify any points in the theories he was working on and elaborating. I have not seen any evidence that he helped any of these patients, and he may have inadvertently caused pain to some.

Going back, as I have made clear, once confirmation bias became the malady that Freud and his followers were ailed by, psychoanalysis developed at a phenomenal speed, in large part by Freud, and, over the first three or four decades of its existence, it enlarged its field of application such that it took over psychiatry and then began to be applied to other fields: literature, poetry, philosophy, art, economics, and medicine. In terms of this last field, psychosomatic medicine became very prevalent, and continues to be to this day in certain countries such as France. Also, as Freud became more and more convinced of his theories, he began to apply them to almost everything around, and began offering explanations in anthropology, religion, archeology, and art.

Along the way, just within the field of psychoanalysis, there were dissenters, but they were soon cut out of Freud's circle. Adler and Jung being the two best examples during Freud's time. Jung, of course, developed his own school, and his theories continue to have many adherents who practice Jungian therapy. In fact, Jung's ideas on synchronicity continue to be much discussed, and we even had a roundtable on the subject at the Philoctetes and the Helix centers. Adlerians also flourished for some time, though one hears less about them today. It may give a perspective on the expansion of Freud's ideas if I briefly discuss a few examples of his works that, in the field, were known as: *Applied Psychoanalysis: Totem and Taboo,* and *Leonardo Da Vinci and a Memory of his Childhood, Moses and Monotheism,* and *Civilization and its Discontents.*

These works, without a doubt, make interesting reading despite the fact that they more or less end up in the same place, namely the importance of childhood sexuality. In Leonardo's case and I am condensing in a few lines a 74-page essay, a memory which Freud, I think, accurately assumes is in fact a fantasy: "I was in my cradle a vulture came down to me, and opened my mouth with its tail, and struck me many times with its tail against my lips". I will not go into the controversy about the translation of vulture and the way it could undermine the paper's thesis, but Freud uses this memory to explain Leonardo's homosexuality, connecting the tail in the mouth to fellatio. He also, additionally, relates the tail to the nipple, and Leonardo's pleasure at having his mother's nipple which also pertains to his ideas of oral satisfaction. Using the facts of the artist's early life, his illegitimacy, his living with his mother for somewhere between three to five years, and then with his father and step mother, and step grandmother, Freud explains the smile on Mona Lisa as the smile of the mother he longed for, and connects the presence of two women in some of Leonardo's paintings to the two mothers or step-mother, and step-grandmother. Furthermore, he also explains Leonardo's homosexuality by the absence of the father in the first three to five years of his life. Finally, he explains Leonardo's intense curiosity and "overpowering instinct for research" as the suppression or repression of the active and constant search for where babies come from.

In the monograph, almost in passing, Freud makes a statement which, to me, is an important contribution of psychoanalytic theory:

"In the first three or four years of life certain impressions become fixed and ways of reacting to the outside world are established which can never be deprived of their importance by later experiences."

As I mentioned above, the paper is 74 pages long, and it contains a great deal of fundamental psychoanalytic theory including matters I have touched on in previous chapters, and additionally, it is rich in demonstrating to the careful reader how Freud keeps confirming his own theories. For example using the case of little Hans "Analysis of a Phobia in a Five-Year-Old Boy," he buttresses his assertions that Leonardo's proclivity for research was connected to the suppression of the sexual part of his childhood research about where babies come from.

Freud ends the paper by a similar statement regarding the effect of childhood experiences which I, again, find worthy of underlining and remembering:

"At the same time we are all too ready to forget that in fact everything to do with our life is chance, from our origin out of the meeting of spermatozoon and the ovum onwards—chance which nevertheless has a share in the law and necessity of nature, and which merely lacks any connection with our wishes and illusions. The apportioning of the determining factors of our life between the 'necessities' of our constitution and the 'chances' of our childhood may still be uncertain in detail; but in general it is no longer possible to doubt the importance precisely of the first years of our childhood. We all still show too little respect for Nature which (in the obscure words of Leonardo which recalls Hamlet's lines): 'Every one of us human beings corresponds to one of the countless experiments in which these *ragioni* of nature force their way into experience.'"

I will now try to tackle Freud's *Totem and Taboo* with the subtitle: "Some Points of Agreement between the Mental lives of Savages and Neurotics." Freud described it as "a first attempt on my part at applying the point of view and the findings of psychoanalysis to some unresolved problems of social psychology." He was making a point by contrasting his work with Jung's work, which, he described as an "endeavour, on the contrary, to solve the problem of individual psychology with the help of material for social psychology." In other words, his disagreement with Jung was an impetus to this work though his interest in archeology and anthropology went back some 15 years. The work was published in 1913, but Freud began his research some three years earlier, and as anyone reading the essay can see that he did do extensive research. In fact, it is only the fourth chapter of the work which contains most of the psychoanalytic ideas. In this regard, it resembles the work on *The Interpretation of Dreams,* which also reviews all the existing ideas and literature before tackling the psychoanalytic discoveries. I should add at this point that anyone who is willing to go through the *Standard Edition* of all of Freud's work is bound to recognize that he was a good writer, and one who grabbed your attention even when not discussing psychoanalysis. He was also a prolific writer; I cannot think of many who have as extensive a literary contribution as Freud, and it is for this that he won the "Goethe Prize" in 1930, which Anna Freud collected on his behalf.

According to Ernest Jones, his biographer, Freud was rather proud of this essay and considered it one of his best. Clearly, he put a lot into it since he was tackling issues that went far beyond the couch, and attempted to explain matters that touched on human behavior, customs, and beliefs on a broad scale.

Naturally, my purpose is not to discuss the whole work but only the psychoanalytic ideas which are primarily limited to chapter four. Here, starting with Darwin's idea of the "primitive horde," Freud describes a father who throws his sons out and keeps the women with him. The sons then kill and devour the father in order to take possession of the women. Freud bases the devouring of the father on the ritual of killing the totemic animal and then eating it. He then asserts that though they killed the father because he was an obstacle to their desire for power and sex, they suffered because they simultaneously loved and admired the father and, consequently, suffered from remorse which gave rise to a sense of guilt. Here is how Freud describes it:

"A sense of guilt made its appearance, which in this instance coincided with the remorse felt by the whole group. The dead father became stronger than the living one had been—for events took the course we so often see them follow in human affairs to this day. What had up to then been prevented by his actual existence was thenceforward prohibited by the sons themselves, in accordance with the psychological procedure so familiar to us in psycho-analyses under the name of 'deferred obedience.'

They revoked their deed by forbidding the killing of the totem, the substitute for their father, and they resigned its fruits by resigning their claim to the women who had now been set free. They thus created out of their filial sense of guilt the two fundamental taboos of totemism, which for that very reason inevitably corresponded to the two repressed wishes of the Oedipus complex. Whoever contravened those taboos became guilty of the only two crimes with which primitive society concerned itself". Freud is here referring to murder and incest (p. 143).

Obviously, most of this aspects of Freud's construction is not based on real evidence but is extrapolated from what he assumed were the desires of little boys, and he used the data from the analysis of "Little Hans" which I have described in the chapter on "Infantile Sexuality." That data, which buttresses Freud's pre-existing conclusion of the "Oedipal Complex," is that the son hates his father and wants his mother to himself—which he thinks he can achieve if his father dies. In other words, he wants his father dead in order to have his mother to himself. In this oedipal triangle situation, he fears retaliation but, because he also loves his father; he feels guilt, and therefore displaces the hostile feelings onto something else, thus diminishing the fear of retaliation and the sense of guilt.

Many years later, in the last years of his life, Freud tackled another subject which was once more far from the couch and can, in a broad way, be seen as a continuation of his work on totemism. *Moses and Montheism* was not published until 1938 when Freud was already in London. It seems that he considered it more as a novel though he applied, once again, the insights he had gained from individual analysis to a much broader subject. Using the facts of Moses' birth in a noble Egyptian family and his espousal of the monotheistic belief of *Akhenaten* in the form of the deity *Aton*, Freud postulates the worship of a second Moses with different ideas and a different deity, namely *Yahveh* at a later date, as a way of paying penance for the murder of the first and the gradual transformation of *Yahweh* into the god of Moses, and the creation of one all-powerful God. However, Freud goes further and, bringing in his hypothesis from *Totem and Taboo* about the killing of the father and the ensuing guilt, he asserts that the return of one God, the Father, represents the attempt at paying (redemption) for this crime by resurrecting the murdered father in this one God. I will not delve further into this hypothesis, but only mention that Freud also applies this notion to "original sin," and the redemption-by-the-sacrifice-of-a-victim to the religion founded by the Jewish Paul, namely Christianity.

I am poorly summarizing a work of some 130 pages, but for my purpose here, I hope it is clear that we are dealing with a work of pure speculation, where, once again, a theory he invented not only explains human neurosis and character, but in fact offers us a key to unravel the whole question of man's need for religion and God. He, in fact, continued this line of argument in a number of other works such as the *Future of an Illusion* where he asserted that religious doctrine is an illusion, and that only science can lead us to the truth (by truth I mean what is factual), and the more extensive essay, written a couple of years after, on man's history, which is *Civilization and its Discontents.* These works, along with his essay on "Why War?" reveal Freud's increasing preoccupation with larger issues than the clinical. As I commented earlier, they show how he became increasingly convinced that the discovery of the two instincts, sexual and aggressive (sometimes death instinct), the inevitability of the oedipal situation, and the expression of these instincts within the triangular relationship of father, mother, and child gave him the tools to understand matters way beyond the couch: art, religion, society, war, literature. It is thus that civilization, to him, represented the need to control and possibly tame the two instincts: sex and aggression, and killing and murder. A control which, while humans need it, they are also unhappy and constrained by, and hence, the discontent.

I need not go any deeper into the works I have very briefly discussed here, they assuredly make very interesting reading, as do works like "Jensen's Gradiva" or "The Uncanny," and they all demonstrate Freud's admirable skill as a writer, and as someone who could keep readers' curiosity active on almost every page.

Suffice it to say here, that all these works and the theories and explanations they offer have lost their applicability and their relevance today.

Naturally, religion not being a science, the arguments Freud presents can be subjects of debate and discussion, but as to the anthropological, social, and psychological theories, it would be hard to find confirmation for them. I think these works, taken together, go a long way in demonstrating how a theory that in its origin is based on speculative ideas, finds confirmation by the inventor of the theory who then keeps finding evidence of the accuracy of his or her assumed discoveries (confirmation bias), and gradually sees it as applicable to a whole slew of problems and observations. One is tempted to ask: Are there other such ideas, beliefs and convictions currently in our world that we accept in the same way but which are no more than an illusion? Clearly, having explanations and theories do help diminish the anxiety of the unknown, and assuredly, anything that decreases fear is always powerful, the other side of it being that there is nothing more powerful than fear and it is possible to think that much of what religion and civilization have tackled—and only to some degree achieved—is the silencing of fear which, nevertheless, is always at the ready to take control of our minds in full force.

In closing this chapter, I would say that the works I have mentioned here, similar to a lot of not only late nineteen and twentieth century writings but to scholarly writings going back many centuries, make not only for good reading as already mentioned, but also help to broaden the mind, fill it with food for thought, and thus make life interesting and rich, irrespective of their accuracy. There are many theories from various fields of study that offer explanations for the same issues Freud was applying his theories to, but, the fact remains that many, if not all, of these explanations continue to fall short of a complete understanding of problems as large as civilization, religion, art, beliefs, prejudices, man's ability to destroy, and every other major matter that applies to the human race.

REFERENCES

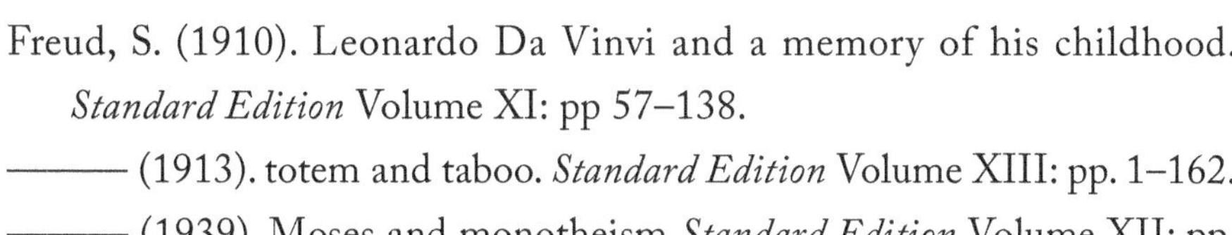

Freud, S. (1910). Leonardo Da Vinvi and a memory of his childhood. *Standard Edition* Volume XI: pp 57–138.

———— (1913). totem and taboo. *Standard Edition* Volume XIII: pp. 1–162.

———— (1939). Moses and monotheism *Standard Edition* Volume XII: pp. 7–137.

CHAPTER 14

Where We Are Today

The building at 82nd Street still stands there. It looks even better than when I started at the Institute. Inside, a recent renovation has created a simple and tasteful lobby. The auditorium, a floor above, was also renovated some years back, as I mentioned in an earlier chapter, and has modern amenities. The third floor that used to be administrative offices originally, was then renovated by Mr. Levy to accommodate the Philoctetes Center, and was recently renovated to create individual offices for rent to therapists. The last floor has not changed much and is rather shabby, nor has the library. Freud still resides there by way of his sculptures and paintings. There is only a part-time librarian, compared to at least two full-time and two part-time librarians when I was a student. The feel of the building has changed however, it no longer feels like our analytic home, but rather, it is more impersonal, like a place you visit.

There is much else that is different, however, and that difference is what this chapter of the book is about.

When I began my training in 1972, there were eight or nine of us. All physicians, and all having completed our second year of residency in psychiatry. There was only one very smart PhD graduate in psychology, but he was considered a research candidate which meant he could not treat patients in psychoanalysis. Over the years there had been a very small number of research candidates, and my guess is that although not sanctioned by the Institute or the American Psychoanalytic Association, they practiced anyhow. As the years passed, the number of students declined but fortunately, following a lawsuit brought by a group of psychologists, we were ordered to accept PhDs in psychology for regular, full training. Not all the members of the institute, especially the more senior members, were welcoming of this change, and they strongly disagreed with the settlement worked out by the IPA and APsA, and being the third group being sued, had very little choice but to go along with, unless we were willing to spend large sums of money on lawyers to pursue the battle to courts. These members strongly believed, and had examples to buttress their position, as to why it was important to be a medical doctor. As the reader can imagine, the main argument was that a non-MD psychoanalyst may miss the presence of neurological or other physical reasons for symptomatology. I remember, as an example, a few years ago, I received a call from a woman who said she was calling to see if I would see her husband and treat him for what seemed like a lot of anxiety. When I asked her to tell me more, she told me that they worked together and that sometimes, in the middle of work, he would sit down and appear confused and not be able to do anything. On one or two occasions he even became incoherent and had difficulty speaking. I told her that it seemed to me we were dealing with a situation more for a neurologist than a psychiatrist and I suggested she take her husband to the emergency room. I heard two days later, that he had been diagnosed with a brain tumor. Of course, such examples are not common, and while I have had to make recommendations to patients about seeing various physicians, the example I cite is the only time where there was a serious and urgent problem.

For a good number of years, the combination of MDs and psychologists still filled the classes but that began to change too. The number of physicians and psychologists applying began to decline. In the 1980s and 90s there had been debate about teaching psychotherapy in addition to psychoanalysis, especially as the teaching of psychoanalytic psychotherapy in the psychiatric programs was declining. At the institute, a very small minority were in favor, but others considered it heresy. Nevertheless, by the late 1990s, it became clear that such a program would be a possible way of attracting students. The hope was that after a year or so of attending the psychotherapy program, they would see the value of the method and apply for full psychoanalytic training. In addition, after lengthy debate, it was decided to accept as students people who had a PhD in social work. Recently the decision was made to accept MSWs as well Nurse Practitioners. Simultaneously, the argument that applicants should not be, at the very most, older than 40, no longer held, and older applicants were accepted. The decline in the number of applicants, nevertheless, continued. This created increasing financial pressure for the institute because it meant less tuition income and less new due-paying members. Simultaneously, the members were aging and no longer paying for dues, and then others were dying. The less money there was, the more liberal the Institute and its admissions policy became, and the less rigorous its education.

The same thing was happening at the national and international level. Life members were increasing in numbers, paying less dues, or no dues, and new members were scarcer. One consequence at these levels was the same as at the Institute level: A liberalization of views, and attempts at creating alliances with other institutes and psychoanalytic organizations that had been shied away from, and occasionally battled with, for years. The rigidity integral to the maintenance of standards began to soften, and the rigorous nature of the training, the selection of applicants, and the requirements for membership, all eroded. Certification in Psychoanalysis, which was created in the early eighties if my memory is correct, and which was a source of major heartaches for analysts who were turned down repeatedly and could not be certified (which did not mean much except that they could not become Training Analysts), became much easier to obtain. Of course, many saw these changes as a felicitous development, because so much unnecessary time and emotion had gone into the fights within and between the Institutes—the national and international organizations on these issues—that it was nice for all who called themselves psychoanalysts to be on the same side and fight for the survival of psychoanalysis.

In the process, psychoanalysis began to resemble less and less like my active years in the field, and while the comfort of having all-encompassing theories, Freudian, Kleinian, Winnicottian, Sullivanian, Bionian, Lacanian, etc. into which every person could somehow fit remains, increasingly there has been a move away from the doctrines, more questioning of them, and a more theoretically flexible psychoanalysis has begun to emerge. There have also been attempts by some, such as the Neuropsychoanalysis group, which I was a founding member of but later took my distance from, to find complicated, and at times not highly sound, ways to keep Freud's ideas alive, while explaining them in a way that could appear to be neuroscientifically sound. I do not wish to engage in these line of debates because I find that in re-framing Freud's ideas, they come up with notions that have nothing to do with the original concept except through the name. Additionally, most psychoanalysts have no interest in neuroscience at all. Any hope of psychoanalysis moving in a more scientific direction is dashed. Along the way, psychoanalysts have abandoned their reserve and have become openly engaged in political debates, discussing their views on the websites of the psychoanalytic associations. Whereas in my time, a psychoanalyst kept his views to himself in order not to contaminate the neutral stance so precious to the analytic technique, no such discretions remain. Analysts criticize each other on the web, express political and other personal opinions, and appear to be feeling that they are changing the field for the better. They may be, but that is only because not much of Freudian concepts are left.

What is happening to psychoanalytic organizations is no different than what has historically happened to other such groups. A certain exclusivity and specialness, often accompanied by rigidity and dogmatism and, in the case of psychoanalysis, a total conviction and reliance on a theory that can be used to explain human behavior, societal behavior, the course of history and religion, etc. After a number of years of self-reinforcing success, and therefore immunity to change, the group is suddenly confronted with circumstances that force change. Unfortunately, often, by that point it is too late, and change becomes only a temporary band-aid. Financial difficulties not infrequently play a role as does the sense of "How did this happen to us?" or "How can we still cling to what we have and not loose everything?"

I was fortunate or unfortunate to be elected to the Board of the International Psychoanalytic Association. It is a two-year term, and you can get a second term if you run again. In that role, I had to attend the twice-yearly Board Meetings which lasted, if I remember correctly, three days and, depending on the committee to which you were appointed, attend the meetings of those committees. I was appointed on the Finance Committee from the US region. The IPA had, at the time, three main regions, U.S., Europe, and South America.

I remember that prior to the second Board Meeting, I decided to look carefully at expenses, especially those of Committees and study groups. I found out that there were somewhere between 80 to 90 of them. A Study Group would be appointed to deal with a specific issue, and for a specific time, let's say two, three, or four years, and required to give a report. Many of these groups continued for years and never gave a report. I also found out that even though all the members of the finance committee were in one place during these Board Meetings, the Finance Committee would not meet, but rather meet in another location at another time. So when we had a meeting in Toronto in July, the Board met but the Finance Committee was scheduled to meet in September in Barcelona. For all these meetings, all your expenses were paid, travel, lodging and food. Between these unending Committees and Study Groups, and these meetings in different parts of the world, the IPA wasted huge amounts of money that could have gone into research. I did not campaign to get re-elected for a second time, and was relieved when

I was not re-elected. Clearly, the organization was calcified. It repeated the same thing almost like a ritual, year after year, with no significant advancement despite some efforts by a small number of the Presidents of the Association. I sarcastically—perhaps too sarcastically—said it was like a travel organization. You became an officer or ran a committee and saw the world at the IPA's—that is to say the membership's—expense. I write this, because this happens in many organizations that eventually fail, and though the IPA is still surviving, I cannot see how long it will be able to continue. The one option they have, and that is true of all psychoanalytic organizations, is to bring down the standards, and widen the pool of applicants to training and to membership, using the strength of the moral argument that now we are better because we are more inclusive, and seeing our many past mistakes and elitist behavior, we are moving towards a more open attitude; it, nevertheless, cannot exist for too many more years. We are currently in the phase where we are still holding on to the unscientific fundamental ideas while claiming that they are being modified and improved through the inclusion of different views and perspectives. However, in my view, with no science, what you try to hold on to will eventually fade away, gradually, yes, but nevertheless fade away.

Over the centuries, empires, dictatorships, social groups (nobility), and religion, to name a few, have followed the same path. Rigid communist regimes, trying to survive by relaxing the controls, softening the dogmas, opening avenues of discourse and descent, then falling.

A faith even befalling the Catholic Church. A year or two ago the Catholic Church proposed closing a number of churches in New York. One of the churches mentioned is two blocks from me. It is a beautiful church called Saint Thomas Moore. There were loud objections to this, and I don't know how it was left off. The Catholic Church that once built new churches all over the world, was now obliged to close some, and maybe sell the real estate in order not to run out of money.

In the case of psychoanalysis, its success as well as the opposition it faced from the beginning led to a conviction amongst us psychoanalysts that we had to defend it no matter what. Unfortunately, this led to a closing of doors and windows to new ideas and developments in science. Furthermore, the conviction that psychoanalysis had all the answers, or almost all, led to formulaic interpretations offered to patients with no questioning of their accuracy or effectiveness and, consequently, of little need to scientifically test them. Here is an example about a case presented at a meeting: the patient talks about how that morning her phone rang and it was her mother in law, and how little she enjoys conversing with her and listening to her various complains. The analyst interprets that the fact of the phone call and hearing someone without seeing them as a primal scene fantasy (Freud has described that children have fantasies about what the parents do in the bedroom when they hear noises coming from it). So this analyst felt he could then analyze this patients primal scene fantasies based on this report of a phone call. It seems almost unreal, but one or other versions of such interpretations, namely, an interpretation that is directly connected to a theory Freud had about childhood development and its ongoing influence in adults, were given to patients all the time. Oedipal issues, penis envy, anal issues, separation anxiety, and so forth.

Over the years, and specially in the last ten to fifteen years, there has been some decrease in such formulaic interpretations, but they have not stopped. In a certain way, they can not stop because either one applies the theories of one of the psychoanalytic schools or one doesn't, and if one is a psychoanalyst of whatever orientation, one applies the theory, because if one doesn't, then what does one do? It is difficult to totally condemn the rigidity, the lack of interest in anything but the psychoanalytic theories, the convictions, the cult-like atmosphere, because it is also those things that helped psychoanalysis survive and, in the fifties and sixties, to thrive. An openness to other scientific findings may have ushered in the current situation sooner but we need to keep in mind that it was only in late seventies, and then on, that gradually the brain sciences began to advance to a point where they could speak of mental functioning, and I don't believe they have influenced many psychoanalytic thinkers of today.

All this to say that yes, psychoanalysis is in serious decline, and that Freud's main hypotheses, as I hope I have demonstrated, are no longer valid. The end of Freud's psychoanalytic theories has come, and there is no way of saving them, but does that mean the demise of psychoanalysis? Will all the ways the institutions are trying to inject life into psychanalysis succeed or just precipitate its total downfall? Are we dealing with a sinking boat and thus the end of psychoanalysis or is it just the end of Freud? Is there nothing from Freud that is still useful?

As I read some of the discussions and emails on the web amongst those psychoanalysts who engage in such communications, we are headed toward, if not already at, a situation where every practitioner—and as I have written, the qualifications are quite broad—does what they deem to be appropriate and applies an existing theory, or their own, to explain and justify it.

The question then is this: Was psychoanalysis (Freudian, Jungian, Kleinian, Bionian, Lacanian, Winnicottian) a useful treatment for all those who engaged in it, and spent many years and large sums of money? I do have many success stories; not all my analyses were successful but many were. So how do we come to terms with this? I also have my theories or explanations; they are not attached to any of the schools I listed, and they are totally unverified, of course, but they are my attempt at explaining the results and changes I, and my patients, observed. How and why did those changes occur? Were they totally unrelated to what we were doing? It's possible, but nevertheless, I would like to discuss my understanding of how this happened, and why many analyses I conducted (and I am sure that other's conducted), were, by and large, rather successful, some incredibly so, in the next chapter.

CHAPTER 15

Psychoanalysis as Treatment

I began work with my first analytic case in late 1973–early 1974. She came five days a week, and I had one hour of supervision per week. She paid me one dollar a session. Six months later I began my second case, again a female, and she had a slightly better financial situation so she paid me $2 a session, again, five times a week. Both patients were sent to me by the New York Psychoanalytic Institute's Treatment Center, which meant they had undergone a thorough evaluation before being referred. My third case was a private case, as the rules at the time were that after taking on two patients from the Treatment Center, we could begin seeing a private case. Of course, all treatments had to be under supervision. My third patient had a great insurance, which existed at the time, so he paid $35 per session, five times a week.

I sat behind the patient who lied on the couch. I wrote as closely as I could, word-by-word, what she said. I tried to make sense of it, aware that the idea of the psychoanalyst listening with a free-floating attention was an ideal hard to achieve with a notepad on my lap. However, supervision required I have notes to remember what I had heard, and my first two supervisors actually wanted me to keep detailed process notes that I read to them once a week for them to guide me. In the session, I tried to make sense of what was going on in the patient's life, understand her emotions and her doings, and then put them through a Freudian lens. Always, specially, in the early days, aware of the Supervisor and worried he may think I said something wrong. Naturally, I was not totally green in the work, having started in the first year of residency, and during the three years I had been supervised, I had learned how to do psychotherapy. In those days, psychotherapy was psychoanalytic psychotherapy, by which it was meant that the understanding of the patient was based mostly on Freud's theories, but the technique did not include the couch and four-to-five-times-a-week frequency. The patient only came between one and three times a week, and was not asked to free associate. My first Supervisor at the Institute was a man, and after a while I felt that he had a certain idea and that whatever I reported, it somehow fell in that frame. My patient, after the first few months, began falling asleep on the couch, and I tried to figure out what it was she was avoiding by it. He said, she is working night shifts so she is tired. To this day, I don't know if he was right or if my formulaic assumption about it being an avoidance was the more pertinent issue, however, I know he was correct in reminding me that you cannot forget reality, and that the person has a life outside the analytic hour. Fortunately, I did not encounter this problem after this first patient. For my second patient, I had a female Supervisor who wanted to hear every word of my notes and who always tried to help me see the patient and her issues in light of her history, and was not much into seeing her via our analytic jargon. This patient remained in analysis for four years, and stopped the work after getting married and moving out of New York City. Many years later, through someone I knew, she sent a message about how helpful psychoanalysis had been to her. After my third case, a man, who had been in analysis for two years, I was given permission to do independent analysis, meaning without a supervisor, however, I decided to choose to be supervised privately by Charles Brenner, and the patient was a woman in her early twenties. By the late seventies, given all my analytic patients and the number of hours, my practice was more than fifty percent classical psychoanalysis, and the rest mostly twice-a-week psychotherapy. The balance tilted in the 80s and 90s as three quarters of my work was psychoanalysis, four to five times a week. I worked 12 to 14 hour days, and saw a minimum of eight patients in psychoanalysis.

All this to get to the point of this chapter. If Freud was wrong, then how did these patients do? I did fail a number of times. In one case, a highly motivated woman patient who came every day for a 6:50 am session, five times a week, decided to stop rather abruptly after 5 years, two months after I had returned from my month-long summer vacation. She did not offer much explanation except for saying that she was not getting anywhere. A few weeks later, I received a call from a resident in a psychiatric unit, asking me about her. She had been hospitalized after a serious overdose. When I offered to go visit her in the hospital, the resident informed her and she refused.

Another man, after almost four years, told me during one session in early November, that on the first of December he was stopping. We both knew he was in the middle of his analysis and had quite a bit more work ahead of him. On the first of December, he did not show up and I never heard from him again. These were the most difficult cases for me to explain what happened. There were another few cases where the patient would try it for a few short months and come to the conclusion that this method of treatment was not for her or him, and stop. I did, however, complete some forty or more analyses, and the majority felt that it was very helpful to them, and a good number felt it had changed their lives. The commitment they made, committing 5, or for some 4, hours a week, plus travel time, plus the financial expense was huge, yet many felt it was all worth it. A few wrote me years later, and a few came to see me years after they had terminated their analyses to get help dealing with a specific issue and, without exception, they expressed an appreciation for what they had been able to achieve while in the analysis and in the years following it.

How to explain this? Naturally these were not placebo controlled cases, and the reports were subjective, yet a glance at the way their lives had progressed, and the changes of directions for the better that had occurred seemed notable.

I will now try to describe why I feel that psychoanalysis was helpful. In doing so, I will be presenting my views of what happened and how the patients benefitted. This will reveal my hypothesis and theories about the therapeutic action of psychoanalysis. Others who can probably also boast about the results of their work will have a different hypothesis behind their success. Therefore, it may well be that my explanation is no more than just my explanation, and that what actually led to change is in something that has, as yet, not been clearly defined. In any case, I will present my explanation and the reader will judge. I should clarify at this point that despite many papers published on the subject and many study groups focusing on it over the years, even decades, there has never been a satisfactory explanation for why psychoanalysis works and why some people feel it changed their lives, some feel much better, some feel it was beneficial, and some feel it was a useless exercise.

I feel compelled to make clear that it is possible my assertion about the help an analysand obtained from the work and the analysand's own assessment of it may be quite different. I would say that in my own case, the help I think I received from my analysis was not really life-changing. It did help have the necessary insights to be able to end my first bad marriage, and it did make me feel more assertive, and therefore better able to run my life, and it did lead to my making a much better choice in my second marriage. In the cases where I feel that my patients did well, I am basing it, as I have indicated already, on seeing them after the analysis, or hearing from them or about them. There are those I feel did well but I have never heard from or about, except for those who have somewhat of a public profile. I need to guard myself against fooling myself as I have seen patients who came to me some time after finishing their previous analysis with someone else, and it was clear to me and to them that not much had been achieved. I would not be surprised if their analysts did not feel differently.

With the above in mind, I would very tentatively suggest a different way of looking at early development, one that does not rely upon psychosexual development. In other words I don't really look at things as the result of, let's say, oedipal or pre-oedipal conflicts, but instead assume that the person in front of me is who she or he is as a result of the following significant contributions: genetic, epigenetic—which is gaining increasing importance, and the environmental, by which I mean the relationships in their life. (I will add to this principal list other less common contributors such as neo-natal illness, birth defects, and possibly certain problems during gestation.) All three of these principal elements contribute in a proximate, moment-to-moment fashion to the gradual growth of the brain/mind. As the neuronal connections increase, the interaction with the parents and surrogates and the environment (in reciprocal action with the genetic and epigenetic factors) form the infant's mind. Every step affects the next step, and may even alter aspects of the previous step, thus making us the individuals we are, like our parents and other important people of our early life, and yet distinctly different. For some time now, I have been suggesting in a tentative way that one way to describe what happens is to consider that these many factors create dynamic templates, maps, networks, or using a modern popular concept, algorithms that determine the way the individual thinks and feels and reacts. In other words, the individual's mind is comprised of these maps, which include both explicit and implicit resultants of experiences and especially emotions. It is, we think evident, that the earlier experiences in life when the mind/brain is developing, have a singularly important role in later experiences and, therefore, are a determining factor in these algorithms. Understanding and dissecting these dynamic maps or algorithms would be a possible way of defining psychoanalytic work. In other words, over the period of months and years, and very gradually, the analysand's way of being and seeing the world becomes increasingly evident, and the nature of the experiences and relationships that led to the way the analysand is today become clearer, and therefore accessible to exploration and attainment of insight. Very gradually, it then becomes possible to feel differently and behave differently without actually consciously trying. For Freud, repressed memories played a key role in the way the person was. I don't see it that way, rather I see it that we are constantly responding to what is around us which is what creates our experiences. Depending on how our parents were, how our social group was, how our teachers were, who we had as friends, in other words, based on what our experiences were, we develop certain ways of feeling and being, and these ways can be very adaptive, or they can lead to maladaptive behaviors and emotions. In analysis we analyze the persons' experiences and their effect on them, including and especially, their early relationships, namely with their mothers, fathers, siblings, grandparents, caretakers, and teachers.

Sometimes, in my work in the office, I explain that embarking on a therapeutic journey is like visiting a city (preferring this to the metaphoric description of Freud's train ride where the person looks out the window and reports everything he/she is seeing) one has visited before but has not delved deeply into. Familiarity with the main arteries and sights, and a few of the connecting streets, has allowed one to navigate and partake in the city life, but now the visit is to be for a longer period of time, and for the purpose of living in it. More streets will need to be discovered, more sights, more nooks and crannies. Every discovery will facilitate the next discovery and, after some time, the visitor now a resident, will look back and see how much more he or she knows and how the same destinations can be reached more efficiently, with less worry or anxiety and with an enjoyment heretofore not available or attainable. This is the patient who, after a period of time, looks back at his or her life and sees how it has been less difficult; not so because life does not have its hardships but easier because the person has not added to those hardships unnecessary complications. The patient now sees a continuity in her or his life and therefore looks at the future with a certain feeling of empowerment and control.

This increase in knowledge about the city that is our mind, is never complete and can never ever be complete during one's lifetime. Much will remain outside awareness, including sources of anxiety and fear. While an occasional dream may suddenly reveal a hitherto unknown fear, a great deal will always remain out of our reach as therapist and as patient. At the same time, however, with the new and limited knowledge, we would be navigating our world with more ease and hopefully happiness and gratitude.

A life progresses like a story in a book, by which I mean a novel . The story is only interesting because different and unexpected things happen that keep the reader engaged. An engaging story is when the reader does not know what lies ahead. The same with our lives. When I look back at my own life, it seems to be made up off different chapters, not all directly connected, though I can find some threads, but none I could have predicted. Chance encounters, occurrences, and events can alter the course of things, sometimes in obvious and expectable ways, and other times in ways one could never have imagined. Even the consequences of our well reasoned decisions are unknown to us over time. I have, above, likened the analytic process to the gradual exploration of a city, in this case our mind; but one could say, life itself is the same, exploring and learning and living through more and more happenings with repetition, constancy, and certainty only playing a limited role. In writing these pages, everyone is living through a pandemic which has changed life in significant though hopefully temporary ways. No doubt, some things will remain different, but other things will hopefully return to their pre-pandemic mode; but the experience would have altered something in all of us. All of life is the same way; experiences and events keep changing us, albeit not always in such major ways, and therefore, nothing is predictable, the book has a consistent story but not a predictable one. Analysis occupies a small chunk of someone's life, and when successful it facilitates the navigation of future unknown events and the integration into the person, in a non-problematic way, of new experiences.

Is Freud really finished? The answer, perhaps surprisingly, after all I have said, is NO. Listening to a person over a long period of time, looking at all their life history, relationships, feelings, fantasies, ambitions, failures, and using the journey to help redirect life in a more satisfying direction would not have been possible without Freud. He and Breuer developed the idea that listening to the story was important and could bring about change, but Freud is the one who did, in fact, make it a tool of treatment. He invented the medicine, and the medicine is the detailed exploration of someone's life.

Freud also has had a significant impact in other ways. For instance, the importance of childhood psychological development.

Today we take it for granted that attention be paid to children's feelings, thoughts, fantasies and fears. Parents take children to child therapists at the smallest sign of distress; they organize their lives so the children could have a good life. They worry about nursery schools, kindergarten, after-class activities, in other words, children and their healthy development is at the center of most parents' minds. Freud, and later his daughter Anna, are, to a large measure, responsible for this. True, some things they believed in, taught, and promulgated no longer hold true, but nevertheless, Freud is very much responsible for our attention to the well-being of children.

The same can be said about relationships in general; concern about the other person, worrying about hurting the other's feelings, offering encouragement as opposed to criticism, valuing a high degree of intimacy, for a good deal of our social and relational values, we owe something to Freud and how the application of his ideas, erroneous as some were, have contributed and opened our eyes to human psychology—to who we are, what we feel, what others feel, and how we can contribute to a better world by understanding the other.

CHAPTER 16

Last Words

It was a small garden, maybe about fifty feet long and twenty to twenty-five feet wide. On the south side of it was a large room, a bathroom and a small storage room. There was a small pool in the garden, maybe 12 feet in length, on each side of which there were two L-shaped flower beds. On the north side of the garden is where we actually lived, living room and dining room on the east side, and the bedrooms on the westside. In the middle was a small room which would be considered a den today but at the time we had no name for it. It was where my brother and I played, and my parents occasionally sat on the couch and chatted. This changed in June of 1955 when the room, with its large windows facing the garden, blessed with a bright light and views of the beautiful flowers and flowering trees, very quickly became the sick room. The couch was removed, a bed put in its place. The only other furniture in the room were two chairs; everything else was moved out. As I lay in that bed, sometimes barely awake or conscious, and for days with unremitting high fever, time stopped, and because it stopped, it lost its meaning. Everything turned white: white walls, white sheets, white pillow-cover. My heart continued to beat but when the time stopped, I stopped living. When time stops, there is no tomorrow, and yesterday is the same as today.

It is no surprise that this episode in my childhood left its marks and, I believe, changed me. Some changes did not last for very long. In the short term—four to five years—I was a good student before it, conscientious and achieved the educational goals easily and well. Afterwards, I did less well in school, did not want to do homework, or tried to do it quickly and poorly to go play. I also became worried for a period of time about losing my parents or brother, and I developed some compulsive symptoms such as making sure a distance was crossed in even steps and not odd steps, and other such rituals. Additionally, in the long term, it changed me in at least two ways I can think of. One, it made me aware at all times of a vague feeling of there not being enough time, and two, it made me feel somewhat cavalier about physical illness. Perhaps, if not surely, it had another lasting impact, my becoming a doctor and my intense interest in understanding diseases, their cause, their treatment, their outcome, and of the thrill of psychoanalysis which, at the time, seemed to me was about discovering the cause of the illness in each individual, unravelling it, and, in the process, not only curing the patient but opening new potentialities for their lives.

As to my constant awareness of time, it is true that for most people time is an enigma. By most people, I mean nonphysicists or people well versed in physics who think time is an illusion. For the rest of us, time always moves and moves forward. Once it has moved you cannot make it go back, even by a millisecond. A good amount of time, we are not aware that it is moving but there are times when we know. We say the week went by so fast, or we say the day was so long. The time we live with is this time. Not the physicists time, but our time, and our time is silent and moving, louder and slow, or fast, or in-between. One case where it is almost always fast is when we look back at our lives over the long term, and we say: "Wow, that went by fast!" This passage of time also accelerates. Slow in our teen and twenties, when we are quite aware of it, unlike middle-age, but then it moves increasingly faster in our sixties, seventies, and beyond. It seems like we want to create an average rate of the passage of time. If it moves fast, we want a break from it, we want to take it easy, relax, rest; and if it has moved slowly or stopped, like it did for me that summer of my 11th year, once we are able to, we run trying to catch up by wanting to fill every moment with something. When we are in a rush, time speeds by and seems short, and when we are waiting, it crawls and seems long. Our emotions determine our perception of time which is everywhere and ever-present.

As I am mulling thoughts about time, it will not have escaped the reader's attention that, as I have been writing about the end of Freud, I have also been thinking about the end of my career and even my life. The first is, of course, my decision, and the second inevitable but unknown as to its exact time of occurrence. At the time I was writing these words, I would not have imagined that an extremely close friend of 50 years would suddenly die. A retired surgeon, a man who loved life and retired early to spend time fishing, hunting, travelling, and just enjoying every moment of life, on a Wednesday morning mid-January, walked down the steps of his beloved home, his heart stopped, and he fell to the floor. No one suspected it, he was so full of life and energy and *joie de vie,* and not ill. When I heard the news, I felt a blunt hard object hit me on my side, and an emotional wave of some kind came over me that again, I have no name for. Then some fifteen minutes later, a wave of thoughts about him forcefully pressed themselves on my mind, and which I eventually wrote down. It is difficult to explain how this happened but clearly the thoughts were generated by the emotion and not the other way around, which made we wonder about how often that is the case, namely that cognition follows emotion and not the other way around. Naturally, it is too big a subject for me to tackle but perhaps it has already been tackled by neuroscientists and neuropsychologists.

Going back to how I started this chapter, some people could perhaps connect the two and assume that the end of Freud, and of my career, and perhaps even my life, are related. I don't think so, and, as I have reported in earlier chapters, the recognition of the end of Freud's monumental influence in mental disorders was gradually occurring over some twenty years.

A few words on living and dying may be useful here. As usual these are my speculations but this is nevertheless how I see things. We are born, or already before we are born, while we are still a fetus, everything is about our living. After we are born and we begin to see the world around us, our energies are directed towards the business of life. We eat, drink, relate to others, and are subject to a whole array of feelings. Some of these feelings have names and others don't. But this force that moves us in life is about our survival and of those under our care. We wake up everyday, we eat, go to work, interact with others, end the day and go to sleep to repeat, more or less the same thing the next day and the next day. We are focused and we are alive. We have goals and then we achieve them, and then we have new goals. We get married, we have children, we get our degrees, we choose a profession, we work, take holidays, enjoy weekends and live. All our investment is on life, and though, when we are a few years old, we begin to understand the notion of death, we don't let it occupy much space in our minds, and when we are young, and for many years or decades, we don't give it much thought or even fully understand it. I realize there are exceptions in the severely depressed where life becomes a burden, but for most of us, we are here to live. Then we reach old age or we get a terminal illness, and now everything begins to look different. There is a difference between having a terminal illness and in being old and anticipating death. In the first instance we anticipate death but we are also preoccupied with our illness, and the treatments, and the prognosis. In being old there is no treatment and no prognosis; our time being alive gets shorter by the day. We still cannot fully live and apprehend death, because living means being alive and death is just nothingness, an idea, a something that is going to happen, but that something is nothingness. There is no longer a destination, a trip, a goal. It is the end of everything. No more feeling, no more thinking, no more life. The book of life is closed. We don't live the past and we cannot live the future, we only live the here and now, and with death there is no here and now. Yes, we all occupy a certain space in time. We know some history through its study and read about predictions about life in the future, but we really and truly only know about the slice of time during which we have lived and occupied space on this earth, and when we are no longer alive our ability to have an impact stops. Freud lived from 1856 to 1939, but unlike most of us he occupied, through the impact of the force of his thinking and theories, another 50 years in this world, some would say a lot longer. He was without a doubt a brilliant man. But, even he would have to eventually die, and I have tried to show why this is the end. Only the reader will decide if I am right.

Of major importance to me, however, is the role Freud played in my life. For all of my career his influence has been immeasurable, even in the last years when I stopped thinking in the Freudian way. My professional life, even today, is a result of Freud's influence, not only because his ideas led me to this profession, but also because even when not being a Freudian, I continue to adhere to the practicing model of Freud. Seeing patients four to five times a week, less so in the last few years as I prepare to retire. Freud helped me have a very satisfying professional life, where, through the intense work, people's lives were changed, and for the better. So was my life influenced by it in positive ways. I learned so much about people, their thinking, their feelings, their strengths and vulnerabilities, and the effects of their experiences throughout life on these characteristics, and all these enriched my life. Freud is responsible, for me, and I would say for most people, to think beyond the superficial.

It is a rather unique situation where you enter into someone's life in all its intimate details. You know so much about them, you live their lives with them. It is as if you are given a key into someone's mental home and can follow them to every corner and even showing them parts of their home they did not know were there. In every hour you live with the patient in their mental home, and then you live in the next patient's home. To a degree your patients' joys and sorrows become yours, no matter how you take distance from it. You worry with them about a job interview, a date, a bad marriage, an illness, a successful event, and so on. You are with them in their lives and they are tenants in your mental home. Yet you are not much more than an hour's presence in their lives, with an occasional minute here and there. They have their lives but, in some way, they have a big presence in your life. The method Freud created, which, if stripped to its bare bones, is an intense investigation of a life with a person, over many years, makes it so that you are never really alone. Yes, inevitably patients are curious about you, they fantasize about where you go on vacation, whether you are married, what do you do on the weekends, but these occupy no more than a very tiny space in their lives and minds. It may be that this is because you maintain what we call a therapeutic distance, essentially you keep your life out of the sessions while your patients' lives are the subject of the sessions.

Just as you hope to bring about positive change in your patients, they also change your life and, in my work, my patients changed my life for the better. They opened my mind, they taught me things, and made me appreciate the value in recognizing that we are all humans and yet can have different beliefs, religions, ideas, desires, a whole range of feelings with fear occupying a large territory, we can love or hate, be friendly or angry, be sad or happy but when all is said and done, we are humans and, as such, we can be understood and we can try to change for the better ourselves. Perhaps, it will be through a weakening of the hold fear has on us, but as humans we must deeply recognize that the person we have called our enemy is as much a human as we are. My patients helped me see that no matter what the issues, no matter how unacceptable a conduct or a feeling, with effort, change and improvement are possible, and not just something to aim for but to long for.

Time and the passage of time play a big role in Freudian theory and psychoanalytic practice. Starting with birth and the oral stage, through anal, oedipal, latency and adolescence.

These stages are delineated in time, orality first 18 to 24 months, anality after that, and by the age of four or so, followed by the oedipal phase, long considered the most important phase by the so-called classical psychoanalysts. Each of these developmental stages is assumed to determine who we are and will be, and to cause lifelong conflicts. Time also plays a role in the practice of psychoanalysis, 50-minute sessions, trying to understand the meaning when a patient comes late or too early, the length of time an analysis lasts, very very rarely less than four or five years, and usually much longer. Supervisions also lasted 50 minutes, though some supervisors were more flexible. Classes, on the other hand, as well as meetings, lasted one-and-a-half hours. Because of the rigidity of the rules about length of sessions, classes, and meetings, time is ever-present in a psychoanalyst's practice. Even vacations, for the majority of analysts, took place in August.

In psychoanalytic theory, time does stop. This is where the notion of "fixation" comes into play. For example, a fixation in the anal stage of development, that is to say, a stopping of the movement forward in maturation, would be seen as responsible for symptoms of Obsessive Compulsive Disorder. This is why having described the notion of the dynamic unconscious, the repository of what is repressed, and the resultant fixations, Freud asserted that the unconscious is timeless. In the unconscious there is no movement of time. What this means is that the conflicts you had at, for example, the age of three, leading to repressions and fixations at that stage of your development, will be with you all your life, and in some cases be responsible for your particular neurosis. The passage of time has no impact on these, and therefore, Freud said, the unconscious is timeless; put another way, for these conflicts time has stopped.

How about my time in psychoanalysis? It certainly did not feel like it had stopped. As I wrote the above, in fact, time always moved, and we were always aware of time, and very much aware of the past because, and this is how I can put it with some distancing, time stopped for psychoanalytic theory in 1939 when Freud died. Yes, many papers were written, many new schools developed, we had many scientific meetings, lectures, and debates, but at the bottom of it all, it was Freud's theory that reigned. Just as when I was ill in the fifth grade, time stopped and nothing changed from day to day except the usual drinking of water, eating small amounts of soup, taking pills and injections, everything else was static. Yes, morning moved to night, and night to morning, but nothing happened, and nothing moved in my life. Psychoanalytic theory in its foundation did not move, yes, psychoanalysts contributed this or that idea but all based on fundamental Freudian theory. Science has to move and does move. One could argue that Newton's law has not moved but it has led to other insights that have moved and continue to move, and a reader of these pages could see the same with Freud, after all, I am now proposing a way to justify long-term treatment by claiming that there is value in the long-term exploration of someone's life in order to bring about significant change. My proposal only exists because of Freud, so it will not be right to assert what I asserted above, yet I still feel something subtly happened. Freud's ideas did not really lead to a consistent advancement of the science of the mind. Yes, I may propose a justification for treatment but that does not change the fact that the science of the mind did not move forward within psychoanalysis until neuroscience and neuropsychology came into existence and explained certain phenomena very differently and, hopefully, will continue to progress. To put it simply, psychoanalysis became a dead end and neuroscience opened a new road.

Freud is very much alive as to the impact of many of his ideas on society but dead as to his impact on what ills us mentally.

Bibliography

Brenner, C. (1957). *The Nature and Development of the Concept of Repression in Freud's Writings. Psychoanalytic Study of the Child*, XII:19–46.

De Mijola, A. (2005). *International Dictionary of Psychoanalysis*. Thompson-Gale, p. 1183.

Freud, A. (1966). *The Ego and the Mechanisms of Defense*. Madison, CT: IUP.

Freud, S. (1893). *On the Psychical Mechanism of Hysterical Phenomena: Preliminary Communication. Standard Edition* II:6.

——— (1895). *Project of a Scientific Psychology. Standard Edition*, I:295–397.

——— (1900–1901). *The Interpretation of Dreams. Standard Edition*, IV–V.

——— (1905). *Three Essays on Sexuality. Standard Edition*, VII:135–245.

——— (1909). *A Phobia in a Five-Year-Old Boy. Standard Edition*, X:5–149.

——— (1909). *Notes Upon a Case of Obsessional Neurosis. Standard Edition*, X:153–249.

——— (1910). *Leonardo Da Vinci and a Memory of His Childhood. Standard Edition*, XI.

——— (1913). *Totem and Taboo. Standard Edition*, XIII:1–162.

——— (1914). *On the History of the Psychoanalytic Movement. Standard Edition*, XIV:16.

——— (1914–1915). *Mourning and Melancholia. Standard Edition*, XIV:243–258.

——— (1915a). *Repression. Standard Edition*, XIV:147.

——— (1915b). *The Unconscious. Standard Edition*, XIV:159–215.

————— (1918). *From the History of an Infantile Neurosis. Standard Edition,* XVII:7–122.

————— (1920). *Beyond the Pleasure Principle. Standard Edition,* XVIII:38–41.

————— (1923). *The Ego and the Id. Standard Edition,* XIX:12–66.

————— (1925). *An Autobiographical Study. Standard Edition,* XX:40.

————— (1926). *Inhibitions, Symptoms and Anxiety. Standard Edition,* XX:87–174.

————— (1932). *Why War? Standard Edition,* XXII:195–215.

————— (1933). *New Introductory Lectures on Psychoanalysis: Dissection of the Personality. Standard Edition,* XXII:57–80.

————— (1939). *Moses and Monotheism. Standard Edition,* XXIII:7–137.

Furer, M., Nersesian, E., & Perri, C., Eds. (1998). *Controversies in Contemporary Psychoanalysis: Lectures from the Faculty of New York Psychoanalytic Institute.* Madison, CT: IUP, p. 58.

Ledoux, J. (2012). *Rethinking the Emotional Brain. Cell Press,* pp. 653–676.

Lindner, S. (1879). *Das Saugen an den Fingern, Lippen etc. bei den Kindern (Ludeln). Jahrbuch f. Kinderheilkunde,* 14:68–91.

Masson, J. Moussaief. (1985). *The Complete Letters of Sigmund Freud to Wilhelm Fliess 1887–1904.* Belknap Press of Harvard University Press, pp. 15–272.

————— (1995). *Some Reflections on Curiosity and Analytic Technique. Psychoanalytic Quarterly,* LXIV(1):113–135.

www.ingramcontent.com/pod-product-compliance
Lightning Source LLC
Chambersburg PA
CBHW061509050726
47593CB00002B/507